Alone in the Backseat

A Memoir

Jennifer Lourie

IDES OF
MARCH

PRESS

For my parents who gave me the greatest gift
a parent can give: self-confidence.

Contents

Contents

"I always feel better with something hard between my legs."

"Do not age. To age is a sin. You will be criticized. You will be vilified. And you will definitely not be played on the radio."

- Madonna

Acknowledgments

This book is basically a love letter to those in my life who have influenced me in some way or made my life better with their kindness. However, there are those in my life who are very important to me but about whom there is no "story" to tell. Not that we don't have stories, they are just "you had to be there stories." Some of my best kinds of those stories are with Kim, Keith, Kayley and Kalissa with whom I am my funniest self and whose love and support means everything. Keith, thank you so much for all the help editing. Kim, thank you for always listening to me.

I want to thank Maddie Smith, a young woman I met briefly but who heeded my call for editors. She motivated me and helped me make my book so much better. Thank you so much Maddie.

Angela, who despite being always so busy, has always been there for me when I needed someone to cry to. I love you so much.

Monique, I will never, ever forget the weekend you came to be with me after Alejandro left. Thank you.

To my amazing teachers in the Portland Public School System, what an education you gave me! Specifically, Ms. Kirkwood and Ms. Sarkis who taught me how to think critically, Mr. Romano who taught me how to diagram a sentence, and Ms. Ross and Mrs. Whidden who taught me how to write.

Finally, I want to thank Design Studio for all the work they did on my book design and for their patience with my pickiness down to the very last pixel.

Prologue: How to Write a Memoir in 36 Steps

1. As a child, sit on the couch with a pile of photo albums while listening to records on giant headphones. Look at pictures of yourself when you were baby and a toddler and make the executive decision to never forget anything.
2. When you are in fifth grade, have the foresight to decide that you are never, ever going to care what people think of you and that you are going to be yourself, always.
3. Read a lot of books. Make sure to read the one that has

the character who keeps a journal. Decide that when you turn sixteen you are going to copy her.

4. Painstakingly keep that journal starting on your sixteenth birthday. Spend hours and hours and hours of your life writing down everything you do.

5. Read more books. Read biographies. Read about how John Adams and Thomas Jefferson and Abigail Adams wrote and saved letters. Learn that because of this there was a ton of primary source material for their biographers to work with hundreds of years later.

6. Write a lot of letters. In addition to spending hours and hours and hours writing in your journal, spend hours and hours and hours on correspondence.

7. Make photocopies of all the letters that you send so that you have a record of everything you wrote.

8. Think about how these photocopies will make your biographer's life so much easier if you ever have a biographer.

9. Fall in love easily.

10. Have your heart broken. Many times.

11. Read more books.

12. Live in four countries on three continents.

13. Absolutely say yes Caterina.

14. Say yes in general. Often.

15. Have love affairs in foreign countries.

16. Keep reading.

17. Get a divorce.

18. Be introspective. Take responsibility for your failures. Change. Grow.

19. Be brave enough to be vulnerable.

20. Share your one bedroom apartment with 71 different roommates to help pay your mortgage.

21. Keep writing in your journal even when you really, really don't feel like it.

22. Make friends from all over the world.
23. Have your heart broken again.
24. Read more books. Make sure to read a variety, everything from David McCullough to Fyodor Dostoyevsky to Isabel Allende to Emily Giffin and Jen Lancaster.
25. Start swiping.
26. Go on lots of dates.
27. Keep a spreadsheet of your dating data.
28. Meet Nathan.
29. After Nathan decides you should stop seeing each other, pursue any type of minimal contact you can have with him while respecting his boundaries so that at least you can remain friends.
30. Fifteen months later, say yes when Nathan offers to "chat in person."
31. Write a love letter to Nathan which you don't intend to send but need get out of your head and heart.
32. Keep writing.
33. Realize that you've been preparing to be your own biographer since you were sixteen, that you have thousands and thousands of pages of your own primary source material.
34. "Ignore the naysayers and the doubters." They aren't your audience.
35. Keep writing.
36. Never, ever, ever give up. Remember that you never know *what* can happen.

1 Dear Nathan

Nathan. It is almost a week since I saw you and I am still full of positive energy from being in your presence. You have no idea how much seeing you lifted my spirits. And even if I never see you again, I am so glad that I have one more memory to add to the list of memories I have with you. A newer, fresher one, where I can still feel your skin and hear your voice and see the freckles on your shoulders and remember how it felt to be in your arms.

I can still feel you holding me tightly from behind with your fingers on your left hand intertwined with mine. I can see your face, my favorite face, as I have my head on your shoulder. I can see you watching yourself in the mirror go in and out of me and I can feel your body trembling and your hands firmly on my hips as you watched that and you loved it.

Given that I hadn't seen you in over a year, I had forgotten these things and loved you for your words, whenever I got to read them. Nothing in the last year of not seeing you made me happier than seeing a notification pop up on my phone that I had a message from you. Nothing. And then you were in my apartment. And then you were on my couch. And then you were in my bed. And then you were inside me. And it seemed liked 2016 and fifteen months of missing you never even happened. It seemed like no time had passed since we watched John Oliver and ate pizza at your place and I told you I loved you a thousand times and then said goodbye to you. The most frustrating goodbye I ever had to say. A tearless goodbye because I only wanted you to have happy memories of me and tearless because I could only be happy in your presence.

Nathan. The man I got to go on only eleven dates with before he decided our age difference was a deal breaker. The man who I loved the most for his perfect, proper rejection. He told me he was "committed to this not going anywhere." Harsh sounding, but actually kind. It was clear, concise, and left no room for confusion or hope. I cried uncontrollably the weekend after he told me, before our final, twelfth date. I was so afraid that I would cry when I saw him. I didn't want to. I worried about it all weekend. I didn't want to see him and lose control of my emotions. That crying that once you start you can't stop? I did not want that to happen. But I didn't cry. I was happy. Even though I knew it was the last time, I was happy. Because any moment in his presence was pure happiness and tranquility. No tears.

And then fifteen months later, he was in my bed again. It was like a dream come true. I had prayed for that. I had wished for it. I had had so many imaginary conversations with him about it. And then it happened. It wasn't a new beginning. Nothing had changed. But, I had an eight hour reprieve from missing him constantly, before he was gone again.

I used to be a huge fan of the TV show *Survivor*. Jeff Probst, the host, has some standard lines he uses every season during the game. Because the game is unpredictable and someone who is on the bottom can suddenly be back on top, every season at some point Jeff says, "You never, ever, ever give up on *Survivor*. You never know what can happen." The same is true for life. You *never* know what can happen. With Jeff Probst's voice in my head, this was the mantra that I had adhered to through my divorce, through sharing my one bedroom apartment for the last eight years with 71 roommates since my husband left me, through navigating the dating app world. But, I had gotten lazy with my positive attitude and my hopefulness. And then Nathan was suddenly on his way to my apartment, and I could barely breathe. And I remembered: you never, ever, ever give up. You never know what can happen.

2 Alone in the Backseat

When I was little I had a toy crib in my room and in it my doll slept while I lay in bed waiting for my imaginary husband to come home from his business trip and climb into bed with me. He arrived in the shape of a pillow that I lay my head on and wrapped a leg around and I talked to him and told him how happy I was that he was there. I couldn't have been more than nine years old. But, I already knew that was what I wanted when

I grew up, what I dreamed for my future: a husband in bed with me to cuddle at night, baby in a crib nearby.

On many weekends, my parents would bring me to spend the night at my grandparents' in Lewiston, Maine, a forty-five minute drive from Portland, where we lived. These weekends were full of blueberry picking in the garden, playing cards, watching HBO they somehow magically got for free through the antenna on the TV and eating as many Little Debbie Swiss Cake Rolls as I wanted - a delicacy that was not to be found in my own home. At the end of the weekend, my parents would pick me up and we would drive home on the highway, lined with pine trees, no city lights to diminish the brightness of the stars in the sky. My parents would talk quietly in the front seat, not wanting to disturb me in case I fell asleep. I would lay down across the backseat but falling asleep was not on my agenda. I was too busy looking out the window up at those stars in the dark sky. My imaginary husband was there with me, holding me and looking up at them with me as we whispered to each other. But, I was alone in the backseat. And despite my various long-term relationships and even an actual, *not* imaginary husband, finding myself so often alone in the backseat became the manifestation of the disappointments and failures of my adulthood. This was not what I had wanted, but this is what I got.

I was born in the '70's and grew up in the '80's, back when most families I knew still had parents in traditional roles. I was an only child in a family where my dad worked and my mom stayed home. I played house in my playroom in the basement. I played outside in the woods. I took naps while my mom did the laundry and hung the clothes on the line in the backyard. I looked out my window in the spring and saw and smelled the lilacs growing on the bush outside. It was an idyllic childhood and I wanted to replicate it when I grew up: a house with a yard, a husband, to be a homemaker and to raise a family. In 1983 this was not an unrealistic expectation. But, society changes and economies change and gender roles change and we have to be ready to adjust and deal with reality as it is or we get trapped in an idea that we can't bring to life and we get stuck. We get stuck in bad relationships, in houses that we cannot afford, in jobs that we don't like. So, we must be cognizant of the changing world around us and learn to adapt rather than fight for something we cannot have and cannot be because it just doesn't exist anymore.

It was actually my marriage counselor who made me realize this. She kept asking me questions about my childhood and I felt like I kept having to explain "No, I don't have issues from my childhood! I am very lucky; my childhood was perfect." I thought that only people with traumatic childhoods would have difficulties as adults. However, she pointed out that maybe it was *because* my childhood had been so idyllic, that that could be what was causing me to have so much frustration as an adult and in my marriage. I reflected on that concept a lot. It took me a while to process and react, the idea being so foreign to my way of thinking until then.

At first I thought what she said was ridiculous. How could having a wonderful childhood be anything but a blessing? But, after thinking about it, I realized I really did need to change my thinking and my expectations to match my reality, not my childhood fantasy. I had wanted everything to be just like it was when I was little, but it wasn't 1983 anymore. Things were different now. I wasn't going to be a stay-at-home mom like I had wanted; that was not an economically viable option for my husband and me. I wasn't going to be able to have a house with a yard unless we moved somewhere else.

Those were hard realizations, but the marriage counselor's observation had a very positive impact on me. When I had to start sharing my home with strangers in order to afford my mortgage, I was prepared to accept the situation for what it was and with a positive attitude, knowing that I was doing what needed to be done, in the reality in which I found myself. It also helped me when I found myself single again at 41, entering the dating world at a very undesirable and undesired age. She wasn't able to save my marriage, but she helped me improve my emotional maturity and I am very grateful for that.

The heartbreaking part though, that I really can't think about because it is just too upsetting, is that I still have all my toys and clothes and books from when I was little. They were all stored away in pristine condition, as I always took care of my things, even as a child. I saved everything because I had intended to have a daughter someday who would play with all my toys. I even collected the books from my favorite authors like Roald Dahl and Astrid Lindgren, purchased with my allowance and babysitting money, hoping to one day read them to my own children. Thinking about these things, probably getting ruined in a storage unit in Maine, makes me overwhelmingly sad. So, I just try not to think about it.

3 *Caroline Ingalls*

When I was married and lonely and missing Maine and my grandparents' garden and the garden of my own that I thought by then I would have, I sat in my apartment every night after work and I lived vicariously through the Ingalls. I had loved *Little House on the Prairie* when I was little and was allowed to stay up to watch it. Now I got to watch as many episodes in a row as I wanted thanks to Netflix and adulthood. Sometimes being an adult is good - no one tells you how many hours you are allowed to sit in front of the TV or what time you have to go to bed.

The one thing I never understood on *Little House on the Prairie* was when the mother, Caroline, would firmly tell her daughter Laura, "Stop crying!" Caroline was such a warm and loving mother and Laura only ever cried for good reason. Why did Caroline not comfort her? Why did she just tell her to stop? It never made sense to me. Why should Laura not express those emotions? Why should she not cry? I didn't get it.

Until one day I did.

I cried a lot in my adulthood. I cried from loneliness and frustration in my marriage. I cried when my husband left me. I cried when I got hurt in other relationships. But then I realized, all crying does, if you really let yourself go, is make you look terrible in the morning. Sure, it is healthy and cathartic to have a good little cry. Maybe a five minute cry. But when you cry for hours and hours? Caroline is right.

Stop crying.

Although I still am not sure exactly why Caroline didn't want Laura to cry, as I doubt her concern on the prairie was her daughter waking up with hideous puffy eyes, I eventually learned to follow her advice as best I could and look much better at the office the day after experiencing hurt or disappointment or frustration or anger. Not crying is also less time consuming. When you are not crying you can talk. You can do chores. You can be outside. While sometimes it is definitely necessary to cry, it is usually better to distract oneself and allow for the possibility of something unexpected to happen.

After I stopped seeing Nathan, I cried often but just a few tears here and there. It was strange that the tears came for as long as they did given that we had only seen each other for three months, but I was so frustrated I couldn't be with him and that frustration just didn't go away. I missed going on dates with him, trying new restaurants with him, talking politics with him, sleeping naked with him. My intimate moments with him were some of the best moments of my whole life. The first times we were together we did not even sleep, our relations lasted for not minutes but hours. We couldn't get enough of each other. It was a perfect fit. This was very, very hard to have taken away. But, I followed Carolyn's advice. There were no sobbing cries. I distracted myself as best I could and allowed for the possibility of something unexpected to happen, as it did six months later, the following summer.

4 Goonies Next to Michael

Michael. Michael was my love from the minute I met him. His cousin Niki, my summertime playmate, lived across the street from our beach house. I think I was eight when I first met Michael. He must have been three. It sounds strange that at eight I would have been in love with a three year old so I must have met him later. I just cannot remember ever not knowing Michael since I lived across from Niki and I definitely never knew Michael without loving him.

I loved Michael's blonde buzz cut, his bright blue eyes, the space he had between his front teeth. I loved his dimples. Oh, those dimples! I loved how smart he was, his fierce wit. I admired how he seemed to be able to talk to anyone about anything. He was so funny and confident; he didn't have a shy bone in his body - his perfect, tanned body. I loved how you could see each of his muscles as he played and ran and did handstands on the beach. I thought it was so cool he could walk on his hands! Michael was a charmer, a characteristic I have always found to be very appealing, probably since discovering it in him. I loved how flirtatious he was. As we played on the beach, I wanted to flirt back but felt bashful. I do not have that problem anymore. I emulated the confidence I admired in him and am grateful for his influence.

I learned patience from my love for Michael. I only saw him once a summer because he lived two hours away and he would usually only come for a few days. I had to be patient all year long while I waited for summer to come to see him again. If I missed him one summer, I had to be patient and wait an additional year to see him. I waited. I was patient. And then all of a sudden, I would see his parents' car pull into the driveway across the street and my heart would beat faster as I knew I was about to see him again - swim in the water with him, have handstand contests with him, hopefully be the one to sit next to him as we watched a movie on the VCR. *Goonies.* Next to Michael. That was heaven.

One night, alone on the beach with the stars overhead, he finally kissed me. He was fourteen. I was nineteen. I guess that seems scandalous, but it didn't feel that way after all those summers on the beach together. The next time he kissed me he was sixteen. I was 21. That time we did a lot more than kiss. Those are cherished memories. Five years is a big difference at that age. I was in college. He was in high school. Our lives were in different orbits, just overlapping in the summer. Years passed.

I left Maine. He stayed. I got married. He got his girlfriend pregnant. Summers passed that we didn't even see each other, but there was always Michael. Tan, blue-eyed, muscular, fiercely intelligent Michael.

And then I was single. And it was summer. And I was in Maine, on the beach with Niki. And I asked her, "Is Michael still with that girl?"

"No," Niki said.

No?!

And I asked "Is he coming for the 4th of July?"

"He should be here in about a half hour," she said.

A half hour?!

I was 42. He was 37. The five years meant nothing now. We were both adults. We were both single. I was going to see him in thirty minutes.

Inhale. Exhale. Breathe.

Michael.

In 30 minutes.

And then there he was, walking down the path to the beach. He wasn't so blonde anymore, but he still had those blue eyes and that gap between his front teeth. And those *dimples*. And then there he was, next to me. And we were kids again. And did handstands again. And were in the water together again. And we tried to hide the attraction we felt because we morphed into our old roles when the five years mattered. But they didn't matter anymore.

Twenty years since the last time we kissed, we kissed again. *Twenty years.* I never imagined through all my imaginary conversations with him, through all those moments of patience and pining that in twenty years he would be inside me again, on the hard stairs, my bathing suit pushed to the side. It was just for a minute because we didn't know if someone would come home and because we knew that our families on the beach would be noticing our absence and because we weren't used to being adults with each other, so we cared what they thought. As he said to me later by text:

> The gravity of our past, present and future, our mutual affection, attraction and desire, being unfadable by space and time drew us together again in the most intimate and passionate state of being where we were powerless to do anything but experience each other as passionately and intimately and physically as possible given the brief window of opportunity within our less than ideal circumstances. We seized an opportunity presented to us by the grace and benevolence of the universe to become one flesh, unite our bodies in carnal pleasure and physically, emotionally, and spiritually reaffirm what burns deepest within us individually and collectively: that our affection, desire, passion and longing for each other goes not unrequited. I was drawn into you as you were drawn open for me by the immense gravity between ourselves.

Yeah. That's Michael.

Swoon.

July 3rd, 2016. Twenty years later, I got to sit on the beach next to Michael, kiss Michael. I got to take an evening walk on the beach with Michael, holding his hand, finally, for the first time, take selfies with the light perfectly capturing the brightness in our blue eyes, his turquoise, mine the color of the ocean. He had dinner with me and my parents, sat at the table with us, made us laugh with all his funny comments and stories. Twenty years later.

The next day, I got to spend the 4th of July with *Michael*. I got to lay on the beach with him and watch the fireworks. The fireworks, next to Michael. That was the *best* 4th of July. I was on cloud nine for those two days, in shock that I got to experience a dream that I never imagined would come true.

Two decades. You just never, ever, ever know what can happen.

And then he went back to his life in Bangor. And I went to Camden with my parents for a little family vacation, a single 42 year old on a family vacation with her parents, alone in the backseat.

5 20/20 Through Puffy Eyes

After my vacation in Maine, grateful for my unexpected moments of happiness and joy with Michael, I returned back to my life in DC: a life in an apartment I had bought with my ex-husband. An apartment whose door he shut one last time and upon hearing the lock click I saw every mistake I had made flash in front of my eyes with perfect 20/20 hindsight.

Why was I always angry?

Why was I so stubborn?

Why when he came home from work did I not greet him at the door with a kiss and a hug rather than give him the silent treatment? I wanted to get married young and I had gotten what I wanted, marrying Alejandro at age 25. I had a handsome, stylish, smart, genuine, hardworking husband. Why did I not cherish that when I had it? Why did I get so angry over little things that didn't matter? Why did I want to get a divorce, for example, because he didn't remember to close the medicine cabinet? I had told him to close it a hundred times so him not closing it meant he obviously didn't love me, right? It is embarrassing now to think about. Hindsight. It is hard to see your mistakes when you are making them. Then there is regret, years of regret for behavior I didn't know would cause me to end up alone. And who could blame him? I was a brat: controlling, bossy, inflexible, rigid. But, I am grateful for those lessons. Unfortunately, he didn't know how to teach them to me in a way that I could hear and understand until I heard him shut the door that last time and I understood everything. But it was too late then.

After he left, I was alone in the apartment whose mortgage neither of us could afford on our own. I thought about how hard we had both tried to make our marriage work, one of the reasons simply being that we were financially dependent on each other. We had always talked about how celebrities divorce so easily and we wondered if it was because of their financial independence - they don't *need* each other. They can just walk away. Finally, after eight years of marriage, Alejandro just couldn't take anymore and he walked away from me, my constant dissatisfaction with inconsequential things and threatening divorce over them having eaten away at his love. Now he had to pay for rent somewhere else which meant he couldn't afford to pay me his half of the mortgage; I couldn't afford it on my own. This was in 2008. Yes, 2008, the height of the mortgage crisis and the recession.

Sell? How long would that take? By the time it sold, I would be drowning in debt. That was not an option.

I refused to be financially ruined by my ruined relationship.

Screw Caroline Ingalls at this time. It wasn't until way later that I understood her Stop Crying rule anyway. At this time there were tears. So many tears. Days and days and months and months of tears. Tears on the metro. Tears at my desk at work. Puffy eyes. I became an expert at the tilt-head-let-tear-fall-out-of-corner-of-eye-so-mascara-doesn't-get-messed-up cry. I was a failure. I missed him. I didn't know what I was going to do. There was a lot to cry about. I was 34 and single. I had wanted to get married young because being thirty and single was my worst nightmare. When Alejandro left me I was four years past that. Today I am more than a decade past that.

I had never cared about an engagement ring or a fancy wedding. I had always wanted the *relationship*. When I was little, I watched soap operas with my mom while she folded the laundry and I observed how the characters lied to each other and manipulated each other and I made the decision that I would never be like them. I wanted a healthy relationship based on honesty and good communication. I wanted a happy marriage. That was my fantasy, not walking down the aisle in a pretty dress I would wear one time. That was what I wanted most in life, since I wrapped my leg around my imaginary pillow husband or cuddled up with him in the backseat and looked out the window at the stars. But, the thing I wanted most was the exact thing I did not get.

6 Desperate to live in an awesome location? (or, How to Run an International Youth Hostel Out of a One Bedroom Apartment)

I cried, but I problem solved. I was not about to sell my apartment for a loss and I was not about to go into debt. While I cried, I thought about solutions. There is always an answer if you think about something long enough and hard enough. I asked myself, "What are my resources?" I racked my brain. Teach Spanish on the side? No, that wouldn't be enough money and was too unreliable. Get a second job? No second job would pay enough to be worth not having any free time. I kept thinking about what resources I had. And then I realized: my apartment. My *apartment* was my resource. I had 1,100 square feet and one and a half bathrooms. The problem became the solution.

Luckily for me, DC is a transient city. Young people are always coming for internships or moving here for jobs or leaving and need a place to stay between their lease ending and their plane taking off. I posted an ad on Craigslist. I thought I could get someone for my couch. One person. *Desperate to live in an awesome location?* That was the ad title. Desperate because there would be no privacy. Awesome because my apartment is in a safe neighborhood, conveniently located near the metro, grocery stores, and shopping.

It worked. First there was Harpreet. She came from California. She stayed with me for two weeks while she looked for jobs and a normal living situation. I loved her name. I wanted to just say it over and over. Harpreet. Harpreet. Harpreet. Having a roommate with a pretty, sing-songy name made that strange, new situation in that dark time feel sunnier to me. That was the beginning. February 2009. Harpreet was number one. Tony was number 71.

I bought an air mattress. I bought a foam pad to put on top of it. I bought new bedding. White cotton sheets. A down comforter and a duvet. If I was going to do this, I was going to do it right. If there was going to be a bed in my living room, it was going to look nice. And it was going to be comfortable.

Then there was Florian, Harpreet's replacement. He was coming from Austria for an internship, the first of three Austrian roommates I would have. But, there was also Jasmine. Jasmine was from Thailand. She came for an interview in person after I had Skype interviewed Florian in Austria. It went well; she seemed nice. I was torn. I liked them both. She really wanted to move out of the situation she was in. I felt bad for her, but Florian had first dibs and I was waiting for his decision. I told Jasmine I would let her know after I heard back from him. As I walked her back to the elevator, she took my arm and looked in my eyes and said so earnestly, "I *really* want to live with you." Her grasp on my arm sold me. Americans are so physically distant from each other, but her touch reminded me of the warmth and affection I had had with my Argentine in-laws. I had been so close with my sister-in-law. There was affection, physical touch, walking arm in arm. It was so nice. I missed that. Because of that grasp, I couldn't turn Jasmine down and decided that given the financial situation, if Florian did agree to live with me, it would be good to have both rents. "Well... I guess... you could share *my* room..." I was 35 years old and about to share my bedroom with a thick-accented, assertive stranger from Thailand.

I bought a second air mattress.

It was a good thing I agreed to offer a spot to Jasmine because Florian ended up only staying for a week. Here I was going through a divorce and trying to pay my mortgage and meanwhile, a change in German agricultural tax law resulted in Florian's internship losing funding which caused him to have to change his plans. Talk about the effects of globalization! Who would have guessed that the German agricultural tax code could affect me paying my mortgage? I really liked Florian so it was disappointing. But, Estelle made up for it, a lovely girl from France with whom I became instant best friends.

Estelle was only supposed to stay for a week while she looked for something more settled, but we hit it off so well neither of us wanted her to leave. As soon as we met, it was as if we had never not known each other. I remember on one of her first nights with me, she stood in the doorway of my kitchen while I cleaned up the dishes. We were deeply immersed in conversation when suddenly I looked at her and said, "We don't actually even *know* each other!" We both laughed at how absurd it was to not really know someone you felt as if you had known your whole life.

I bought another air mattress.

Estelle overlapped with Florian so at this point there were two beds in the living room and two in the bedroom. All of a sudden, I was apparently running an international youth hostel out of my one bedroom apartment, confirmed by Tomas from the Czech Republic, the next addition.

These were happy times. I wasn't alone and lonely anymore as I had been for so much of my marriage. Tomas, Estelle and I became like three peas in a pod. Every day we couldn't wait to just hang out with each other after work. Estelle was so sweet; she would greet me with a hug every evening when I got home. She loved taking advantage of American hugs since hugging isn't much of a French tradition. Tomas loomed over us at 6'5", a gentle giant, more like a giant wagging puppy dog. He bounced all over the apartment, arms flailing, as he enthusiastically recounted a story from his day, giving me anxiety that he would break something given that his arm span was almost seven feet wide!

Tomas' favorite activity, aside from hanging out with us, was eating a pint of Ben & Jerry's Cherry Garcia ice cream in my building's sauna upstairs. We thought that was such a clever idea but we missed him during his sauna time. The three of us became inseparable and we couldn't believe how lucky we were that our paths had crossed. We called ourselves the Dream Team. Our time together wasn't long enough and it was heartbreaking when they each moved out, back to their own countries.

Jasmine was focused on her studies so she didn't hang out with us much. However, this petite Thai woman was quite a character whose presence loomed large. Tomas, Estelle and I laughed about how she dominated the kitchen - if she was cooking, no one else was allowed in there with her. We also laughed about the fact that she wore a *shower cap* when she cooked. She took over my room and she took over my kitchen. Her different bottles of Thai seasoning covered practically the entire kitchen counter. Disappointingly, she never offered to share the food that she cooked as she reigned over the kitchen donning her shower cap.

Jasmine ended up moving out sooner than expected to return to Thailand for the summer. She didn't say goodbye when she left. Maybe it was because it was six o'clock in the morning and she didn't want to disturb me? Maybe she didn't like me anymore? I wasn't sure. Maybe that was just the way she was. In the fall, however, I was alerted of her return to the States with this text message, "Jen. Do you want to go to see a free concert at the National Gallery of Art tonight or what." Typical Jasmine. She made me laugh.

Harpreet, Florian, Jasmine, Estelle, and Tomas were the first of many, many roommates with whom I shared my home. I have had 71 roommates from sixteen countries (USA, Austria, Thailand, France, Czech Republic, Jordan, Russia, Belarus, Spain, Nigeria, Canada, China, India, Cameroon, Ghana, Guatemala). The shortest stayed for a night, the longest for two years. At this point I can't even remember how long I shared my own room for. Was it a year? Two years? For at least the first few years there were always four of us in my one bedroom apartment, sometimes more. Sometimes I had an overlap of someone moving out and someone moving in and at those times there would be five of us under my roof. Guests were welcome too so there was even a night or so that there were seven of us! On one of those particular occasions, when every bed in the apartment was full and the couch was accounted for as well, Alexei, my roommate from Russia, had his Belarusian friend Yury come to visit. We decided to turn the dining room table into a fort, covering it with blankets and setting up a sleeping bag underneath, complete with a lamp inside. I felt like a kid again setting up that fort. We laughed so hard at our silliness as we thought of more and more ways to make it cool, like adding a sign that said "Fort Yury" decorated with a Belarusian flag drawn on it. When Yury arrived that night and saw his accommodations, he loved it. He was actually the only one in the apartment who had any privacy!

Stacey, from Kentucky, was another such overlap roommate. I had met her previously when she was selected to be the recipient of a college scholarship from a program I managed at work. She contacted me because she was coming to town to intern on the Hill and wanted to know if she could stay with me, someone in a new city who wasn't a complete stranger. I had liked her when I met her, so, though I wasn't going to have an open spot until three weeks after her arrival, I knew I could handle her being a fifth on the couch until a spot opened up. After her first night however, Stacey couldn't handle the couch. Well, I was already sharing my room, why not my bed now too?

So, yeah, I even shared my bed. For three weeks Stacey slept with me.

These are things you do when you need to pay your bills and if you do them with a positive attitude, they turn into good stories and good memories. They even turn into invitations to weddings in Kentucky where you get included in the family preparations even though you are not in the family and you get to be with the bride while she gets ready. You then get to attend a wedding of four hundred people because the bride has eighty first cousins alone which fascinates you because you yourself only have two. You even get to be so lucky as to have the privilege of staying at her 89 year old grandmother's house for the night, a grandmother to 41 grandchildren. In the morning you get to have coffee cake with this lovely matriarch and ask her what it was like to raise twelve children in addition to fostering a number of others over the years. These are the very special things you get to do when you do what you need to do.

Sirisha also shared my bed. However, unlike Stacey, not when I was in it. Sirisha answered my ad with a different type of need. At seven months pregnant, she was exhausted every day from her long commute to work from the suburbs and back. All she wanted was a place to take a nap during her lunch break. Conveniently, her office happened to be right across the street from my apartment. Every day, Monday through Friday, I would put a separate set of sheets and blankets on my own bed for her and she would come take a much needed nap. On Mondays I would come home to $125 on my nightstand - easiest money I ever made.

Kanru, a college student from China, was roommate number forty. He lived with me his junior and senior years. Although Kanru spent two academic years in Washington, DC, he only went to see the museums ONE time. All Kanru did was go to school and then come home and study. He studied all night long. He barely slept. He was completely exhausted. He would come home from school and just flop onto his bed, passing out for a short nap until getting back up to study through the night. I can't imagine the pressure that he must have been under that compelled him to live that way.

I worried for him about this unhealthy behavior and about the fact that he was completely missing out on making any friends, living in DC and learning anything about American culture. He had perfect English grammar and an excellent vocabulary but, due to lack of practice, his accent was so strong sometimes it was hard to understand him. Despite the language barrier and the crazy study hours, he did have a great personality and made me laugh with some clever jokes. He just needed to get out and socialize and practice his English! I was happy when Arlene, our former roommate, invited us both to a housewarming party at her new place.

Kanru asked if he could bring his laptop.

Kanru socialized a bit at the party, though it was clearly under duress. When he finally couldn't take any more of the pressure of not being "productive," he asked if he could excuse himself to one of the bedrooms to study.

Oh, Kanru.

This only child from Maine, who never needed to share, was now sharing everything I owned with mostly complete strangers. Now I did not have any spot to myself, for a while not even my own bed. I told people about my living situation and they told me they "could never do that." But what would they do in that situation? Go into debt? Give up? I wonder. Was I going to just curl up and lament my circumstances? What would that accomplish? No, I had to accept my circumstances for what they were, live in reality and do what needed to be done as I was confronted with unexpected challenges (like German agricultural taxes!).

Walking down the street one day, I saw a *Keep Calm and Carry On* poster in a shop window. I bought it and had it framed. I hung it up in the living room, a guiding beacon to help me navigate a revolving door of Craigslist strangers sleeping on air mattresses throughout my apartment. Nothing in my life turned out as I had wanted or expected but my plan was to just keep calm and just carry on and that is exactly what I did.

7 Simultaneous Orgasms

It seems like a lifetime ago now, but before I became an expert at sharing my apartment with Craigslist roommates, I met my ex-husband in Argentina. I was there teaching English. Three weeks after breaking up with my college boyfriend of five years, I met the man I was going to marry. I fell hard. We both did. I can't remember now what those feelings felt like. I know I loved him but I can no longer feel the love or the pain at it not working out as we had intended. The feelings are abstract now.

We fell in love, quickly and deeply. We never had to declare ourselves exclusive because from the day we met we were together every day. In the beginning, I was up all night with him every night. I didn't sleep. I don't know how I managed to function during the day. His parents owned a rental property that was unoccupied, so every night, after I had dinner with my host family, he'd pick me up and we would go there and just be together. A mattress on the floor, candlelight because the electricity was off, a romantic secret hideaway - I do remember that like it was yesterday.

I loved his horizontal style. He was slow, sensual and passionate and he cared about my pleasure. He took his time. He told me to relax and that enabled me to truly and finally do so and enjoy. Those were firsts for me. I couldn't get enough. I loved the way he felt, the way he made me feel, the way he made us have simultaneous orgasms when I had never even been able to orgasm from intercourse before. Was this why I fell in love with him? I think it was. Why I married him? Probably. But a marriage needs a lot more than simultaneous orgasms to function. Even after our emotional connection was damaged by dissatisfaction and disappointment, our physical connection in our intimate moments never faltered. Our souls had become unknowable strangers but our bodies remained perfect mates. My married orgasms were often accompanied by tears. A release of emotion - frustration and loneliness. Why couldn't our minds connect the way our bodies did? After we came simultaneously, he would feel my wet tears on his neck, but he didn't know how to fix it and neither did I.

8 Kevin

Kevin. It has been over a year that we have been seeing each other. You were 29 and I was 42 when we met. We went on a date and enjoyed each other's company. When you kissed me, your kiss was impressive. You were a *really* good kisser. I went home with you. You were the first person I was with after Nathan and I desperately wanted to feel with you the way I felt with him. That did not happen. But, a year later, we are still seeing each other.

When I first started seeing you, your very blonde hair was short. You've let it grow out a little since then, long enough for me to tell you that I love running my fingers through your blonde locks. You look good this way.

I don't think either one of us expected this to last as long as it did. The first time we were together you came in two minutes. We took a break. We did it again. You came quickly again. You were Not Nathan and you left me dissatisfied. But, despite your lack of endurance, you still felt really good and you had the slow and sensual style that I like. A few weeks later, I was in your neighborhood and I asked if you wanted to go for a round two. I was in need and I was not invested, so I knew I would be able to relax and get relief if you could just last long enough. You did. Your endurance was much improved. We took a break and then went again. You laughingly told me about how you told your friends what happened the first time and that you hadn't really cared that you left me dissatisfied because you got yours.

Oh really? Was that so?

I stopped riding you, I thanked you and I kissed you goodbye. The joke was on you. We were 3-1, things needed to be evened out a little.

You are my Not Boyfriend. We are in a Not Relationship. You are my body's lover but not mine. We see each other to satisfy needs. I don't know what I would have done without you this past year to provide me that much needed relief, that physical intimacy with another human. I am grateful for you. You give me long, deep, perfect kisses. You are a perfect kisser. We trust each other. You always respond to me when I contact you and you never confuse me. I can say nice things to you, like that I am grateful for you and that I appreciate you and that I love our Not Relationship and I am not afraid you will get scared and run away.

You live downtown so it is convenient for me to come see

you after other plans, like manicures or nights out. We have a routine. We do it once. We talk. We update each other on our lives. We laugh together. We do it again. I leave. Or if we are at my place, you leave. Or, there is a sleepover, but those are rare. On those occasions you hold me all night and it is a welcomed break from sleeping alone. We don't talk to each other much outside of these times. Our communication mostly consists of scheduling. Our intimacy is gentle, soft, affectionate, slow, and passionate. I remind myself that this is not love making, though it feels like it is. But it is not. I asked you recently, given that after a year neither of us had found someone else, if maybe we should consider spending more time together. You said that relationships are fragile and that you love what we have. It makes you happy. You said you think it makes me happy too. I didn't disagree. I do love our Not Relationship. But this is not happiness.

The other week we had tentative plans to meet up at the end of our evenings. When I was done my activity, I messaged you to see if you wanted me to come over. You were still out, but for once you breached the boundary you so strictly enforce - the boundary that has allowed our Not Relationship to function without confusion, that prevented feelings from developing, and you invited me to join you. I was shocked. But I was in! The timing worked out perfectly and I met you and your friends just as you were heading to your next stop. We went to a bar where there was a band playing live music. Your friends were so nice. It was fun and spontaneous. I sat next to you and you were affectionate with me. For one hour, I felt like a girlfriend. I knew I wasn't, but I felt like I was. It was such a nice feeling, one I hadn't felt in a long time.

I enjoyed being with you in public, not taking my hands off you, talking with you and your friends, knowing that soon we would go back to your place and you would give me your amazing kisses and we would be naked and intimate and connected and that I would sleep in your arms that night and not be alone. In that moment yes, I did feel happy.

I was not going to have to uber home that night, alone in the backseat, and I was grateful for that.

9 What would I change?

    I am not going to include the name of my last boyfriend in this book. Handsome, sweet, helpful, intelligent, cool, funny, charming, clever, capable, tidy, loving, cuddly, adorable. Possessive, jealous, insecure, manipulative, controlling, mean, verbally and emotionally abusive. He does not deserve to have his name included in this book, or in my life. We are not going to talk about him. Except to say that I wasted my time. *He* wasted my time. Six years. I regret it. A police officer ended the relationship for me. I did not look back.

Before you turn forty, you feel like you have a lifetime ahead of you. You don't know the value of time and therefore, it is easy to waste. You waste time on stupid fights, in bad relationships, being angry. Then, one day, when you are 41, you are shopping for clothes in Buenos Aires, your favorite place to shop. You started shopping there when you were in your twenties, on trips with your Argentine husband. Back then you admired those beautiful, glamorous Argentine shop girls and you wanted to be like them, to emulate the way they dressed, their long hair, their perfect bodies, their style. But you realize...Wait... It is almost twenty years later now and these shop girls are still the same age. But you are not. And you really *can't* look up to them anymore as your style and beauty role models because you *can't* be like them. They have what you don't have: their youth, their whole lives ahead of them. And then you realize, as you start to notice the crow's feet and the laugh lines, that you don't have your whole lifetime ahead of you anymore. And you feel pressure to make the right decisions NOW because time is flying by and every second that you have left to enjoy you want to enjoy without wasting it, while you can, while you still look good and feel good because... now you are aging.

You remember when you were little how slowly time passed, especially if you were waiting for something exciting, like opening your Chanukah presents. The day dragged on and on until your father finally came home from work and you finally had dinner and you finally lit the Chanukah candles and then after your mom made you sing at least two Chanukah songs, you *finally* got to open one of your eight presents. Those days waiting to open those presents *dragged*. They seemed to take *forever*. Now time flies so fast a year seems like a month, a month seems like a week, a week seems like a day, and if you are with someone like Nathan, a day seems like a minute.

They say youth is wasted on the young. It is true; what I wouldn't give to go back and live my life again with the perspective I have now, now that I know how time flies. I would go back and I wouldn't waste a minute being angry for silly reasons or in bad relationships.

But, if it wasn't for wasting six years in my last relationship, I would not have met Nathan. This has created a loop which plays in my brain as I wonder, was that worth it? Were six wasted years, leaving me today 43 and single worth it for twelve perfect dates? Twelve dates with Nathan, plus one unexpected visit fifteen months later? Since all our dates except the first were sleepovers, that means I got to be in his presence on 25 days. Twenty-five days out of my entire life. Twenty-five moments in which I felt so *happy* and felt pure peace like I had never felt with anyone before. Was it worth it? Probably not.

Sometimes I think about what one thing I would change and what the butterfly effect of that change would be if I could go back. Well, my first response is always a no-brainer: I would go back to high school with my hair iron, eye liner, and Accutane.

But what *one* decision would I choose to change that would end me up in that happy relationship I dreamed of when I was a little girl? Would I not get back together with my college boyfriend Scott after he broke my heart my freshman year of college? Should I not have taken him back and stayed for five years, in the end just loving him as a best friend? I don't know. I had great experiences with Scott. He was my first long-term boyfriend.

Scott with the brown hair and blue eyes. He had a mullet when we first met. How did I have a boyfriend with a mullet?! He was a musician; it was 1992.

But still.

I hated that mullet.

But, he was sweet.

We met in the cafeteria where I was eating lunch alone one day and he asked if he could join me. That afternoon I came home to a note on the whiteboard on my dorm room door saying that he would stop by later. When he did and I wasn't there, he looked for me and found me in the study room. He distracted me from studying and we ended up staying up all night, talking non-stop. We spent nine hours straight talking in that study room. He asked permission before he kissed me for the first time. Guys today never, ever ask permission. I wish they did.

Over the summers we wrote each other letters because that was before email and texting and cell phones. He visited me in Maine and I visited him in New York. His parents welcomed me into their family and I spent a lot of time at their beautiful home in Scarsdale. That was where I heard "The Piña Colada Song" for the first time, during a Christmas break. I was sprawled out on the living room floor, listening to Scott and his older brother play their guitars in front of the fireplace, watching the snow falling outside through the wall-to-wall sliding glass doors. I couldn't believe how clever those lyrics were! I didn't understand how I had never heard that song before! But how lucky was I that the first time I heard it, it was performed live for me by the boy I loved on a beautiful, cozy, snowy day in front of a fire? I am sure I probably made them play it over and over until I knew every word of that sweet story. God, that song moved me. That moment. I will never forget it.

My parents loved Scott. My friends loved him too. I used to wish that I could clone him so that each of my friends could have a boyfriend as nice as mine. There was nothing to not like about Scott. Everyone thought we'd be together forever.

Scott is married now with two kids. I am happy for him; he is happy. We are still friends. I think that could have been me if I had wanted it but he just wasn't the one for me. He is the reason that I know you cannot choose who you love. If we could choose these things I would never have broken up with Scott and I would have had everything I had wished for as a little girl. But, my love had changed to friendship love and I knew it had to end. I don't know if despite the many lovely moments we shared, if staying in a relationship with him for most of my college experience was worth the opportunity cost of possibly meeting someone else. I don't know if that is the thing that caused me to end up spending so much time alone in backseats later in life. It might be, but I don't know. It is impossible to know.

Would I go back and change the fact that I didn't pursue my Argentine boyfriend Alejandro as only a pleasant, shared brief moment as I had done with my French boyfriend Gille who I met when I was an au pair in France? Should I have ended things with Alejandro when my three month exchange program ended and not have pursued a long distance relationship? Should I not have gone back to visit him? Should I not have stayed after the three week visit was supposed to be up? Should I have stayed but let things end when I finally did move back to the States? Should I not have married him? Should I have gotten divorced sooner, after one miserable year instead of nine? Or two or three or five? I am not sure because I learned so much from him and his family and the many return trips to Santa Fe, Argentina. I am a much better person as result of that relationship. I am no longer a brat who wastes time being angry over silly things or is controlling or inflexible or confused about the fact that people are just different – they have different needs, process things at different rates, communicate differently. These were lessons I badly needed to learn. If I hadn't gone through all that I would still be difficult and high maintenance and rigid. I like who I am much better now. But maybe if I had made different choices, I could have met someone who could have taught me those lessons with patience and kindness, helped me grow faster, in a happier way.

These are the things I think about when I ponder all the factors and decisions that ended me up where I am today, when I wonder what one thing I could change to keep me from spending so much time lonely and sad and frustrated and alone in backseats. I think it would be fun to experience my life over and over and over (but with better hair and makeup!), each time making slight changes to see what the different outcomes would be, like in the movie *Groundhog Day*. But, each time I think about this, I circle back to how I felt during my 25 moments with Nathan and I wonder if it would be worth it to go back and change something that would have made our orbits not cross. And then I think, maybe that is just dumb. And I just don't know.

10 Loneliness

Loneliness is one of the worst feelings. When I lay on the beach by myself throughout my teenage and college years I *wanted* to be alone and I never felt lonely. Back then, rejoicing in my own company, I never imagined I would so often experience the feeling of loneliness that I have as an adult or that I would learn that there are different kinds of loneliness. I think the worst kind is in the presence of another. I was so lonely with my ex-husband. I craved his attention, but he was withdrawn. Maybe he was withdrawn because I was such a pain? Or maybe I was a pain because he was withdrawn? When I was married, I thought it was the latter. I thought I was perfect and everything was his fault. But in hindsight, I think it was more the former. Maybe I was to blame for own my loneliness? Who wouldn't withdraw from someone who lived annoyed by little things that didn't matter and threatened divorce constantly? At the end of our relationship when he was physically present but already emotionally gone, I would cuddle up to him in bed, hold him from behind, caress my foot against his as I had always done, every inch of my body touching every inch of his, not knowing how to reach him, wishing things were different, feeling impotent in his silence, incapable of preventing tears from escaping out of the corners of my eyes. In those moments, with my body pressed against his, I felt the worst kind of loneliness.

Given the transient nature of DC, many of the friends I had made when I was in college at American University or later at work had moved away. After Alejandro left me, I was really alone. That was a different kind of loneliness. I wasn't the same girl who had used to wish for beach days all to myself. I didn't *want* to be alone anymore. I had learned from Alejandro and his family and Argentine culture that life is about sharing time with people. They taught me to value time with others as the best thing in life, shared moments of storytelling, laughter and human connection. I am so grateful to them for teaching me that lesson - they changed me for the better. Now I wished for friends. I would walk by restaurants or bars and see people inside laughing and enjoying themselves. I *wished* that were me. Outside looking in, I was literally and figuratively on the outside. I felt like I was always on the outside and I was extremely lonely. It was a terrible feeling.

I worked really hard and put myself out there to reconnect with the few local friends I still had and to make new friends. It took a long time and a lot of effort. I often felt it was like pulling teeth to get people to hang out with me. I didn't understand that and it hurt and frustrated me. When I felt lonely, I reached out to people to let them know I was thinking of them, maybe they felt lonely too? I invested a lot of time and energy into building relationships. I worked hard at being the friend that I desperately wished I had. I called, I messaged, I checked in, I was thoughtful. Sometimes, though, that made me even lonelier because those gestures were rarely returned. However, if they were, it made my heart full. It felt so good to be thought of; I learned how important it is to let people know you are thinking of them. You can save their day, even their life, with that small kindness.

The constant stream of roommates coming through my apartment helped a lot. Having to share my one bedroom apartment with strangers turned out to be much more of a blessing than a burden. I was never alone anymore. It was harder to feel lonely when I had people around me all the time.

But still, there I was, living my worst (first world) nightmare: a failed marriage, six years wasted in a relationship that went nowhere, 41 and single. That was not a position I wanted to be in. What do you do when your life turns out the opposite of what you wanted or expected? Do you dwell on it? Do you stamp your foot and whine that it isn't fair? Sometimes a situation does require a good foot stamping. But stamping doesn't move you forward. You really can just stamp your feet if you stand in one spot. And, if you stay in one spot, you get stuck. Better to give one good, strong stamp and move on.

One thing that helps me is to think about how lucky I really am. It is hard to feel sorry for yourself when you remember that millions of the world's population do not even have the luxury of *toilet paper*. Or, when you are grateful to just have indoor plumbing and that you are not one of those poor women in Africa who have to walk for miles with a bucket on her head in order to have clean water. I like to be mindful of all the blessings I do have and to put positive energy into the universe no matter how down I may feel, as I have learned that gratitude is a habit that uplifts.

A few years ago, I visited my good friend Randon in Ohio and I got to spend a Sunday with him and his family. I wanted to participate in their family culture and to learn about Midwestern Christian family life, so I went to church with them. In the sermon, the pastor talked about having an "attitude of gratitude." I felt proud of myself because that was how I already lived my life, but I was also excited to have a new, catchy phrase for my philosophy. Being grateful and positive does take a lot of effort though and sometimes, when one thing after another is going wrong, it can be exhausting. I admit that I have heard myself complain occasionally that "I am tired of having a good attitude." But what other choice do we really have? I am not one to waste time feeling sorry for myself. I am one for action. So, I give one good foot stamp and then I adjust my attitude and move forward.

11 "Send me an ass pic"

My last relationship was so taxing that once it ended, I relished doing what I wanted when I wanted without having to answer to anyone. I felt like I was me again, felt that bubbly happiness on my insides that I hadn't felt for what seemed like ages. I was single for the first time in a very long time. After all the headaches I had been through, I did not even *want* a new boyfriend. But, I was afraid that my future self at 51 would be mad at my 41 year old self if I didn't hurry up and try to find someone before I was even older and less desirable in this youth obsessed culture where women my age and older are practically invisible. Luckily for me, a life of not drinking or smoking or doing drugs and starting a regimen of Estee Lauder anti-wrinkle cream probably in high school, I still had my youthful looks which I was very grateful for but also c o n s t a n t l y stressed over losing. So, I needed to hurry up and get on with it.

On behalf of my future self, I made my Tinder profile and I started swiping. And there he was. Green eyes and dark brown hair, his smile looked like a movie star smile. Nathan. I was 41 and he was 28, but when I swiped right we matched! His photos were perfect. He was perfect. I wanted to meet him. I wanted to at least go on one date with him, sit across from him and just look at his handsome face in person. I never expected to *like* him. Or to go on multiple dates with him. Or to fall in love with him. He was one of the first people I went out with. And, despite it not working out with him, knowing that I had found him gave me hope when depressingly swiping that if I had found him, maybe there would be someone else of his caliber to find.

The last time I was single, I was 34 and ended up with a 27 year old boyfriend. When we broke up six years later, he was 34, the same age my husband had been when we got divorced. I was 41 and had never been with anyone older than 34! I also had never been a single version of myself outside of my thirties so it was quite a surprise to me when I started swiping that all the age appropriate men looked *old!* When did that happen?!

After a while it got depressing, so I lowered my age settings just so I could see a handsome face sprinkled in among the guys who had let themselves go. I was a very youthful looking 41 and put a lot of effort into maintaining myself. I also didn't *feel* like a 41 year old on the inside. That is when I learned that as you get older, you don't *feel* older on the inside, despite the fact that your appearance begins to betray you, and when you talk to people you start to wonder how they see you because they don't actually see your insides, they see your appearance. You begin to question if your personality and clothes and hairstyle only match your insides now but should be adjusted so that they match your outsides.

And *then* you start to experience something you haven't experienced since you had acne: self-consciousness.

And it is stressful and you hate it.

As surprised as I was about how men my age looked, I was just as surprised, once I lowered my age settings, that younger guys would have their age settings high enough to even see someone my age. And, I was equally surprised that I matched with pretty much every single guy I swiped right on under age thirty. At least it became more entertaining, and it was great for my ego.

I didn't realize how unrealistic it was to think that I might find another boyfriend in his late twenties or early thirties because that was what I always had before. I didn't expect that I would be called a cougar either. I *hated* that. I didn't know that these guys were mostly only swiping for one reason and that few of them would want to actually *know* me. I didn't know how disinterested many men are nowadays in actually making a human connection. I didn't know how badly that despite my youthful looks, my age would work against me. I didn't know that guys in their forties want women in their thirties and guys in their thirties want women in their twenties and that guys in their twenties would all want to bang me, leaving me with lots of matches but seemingly no options for something real and meaningful. I didn't know anything.

I did realize it was probably going to be a lot harder than it had been in the past to find someone so I figured I might as well keep track of how many guys I was going to have to go through before finding a Boyfriend. So, I kept a spreadsheet. I kept statistics. And,

I learned a lot. Most of the lessons I learned I am not better off knowing, but I know a lot about men now.

Did I even want a boyfriend at this point? I thought I didn't. But I don't know if I really didn't. I knew I just wanted to put in the effort to find one so that my even more undesirable 51 year old self ten years in the future wouldn't be mad at me for not trying harder. So, I tried really hard. I swiped like it was my part time job. It was exhausting. And disheartening. And extremely time-consuming. I met some cool people. But were any of them really even worth knowing? Yeah, maybe a few of them were. Nathan certainly was. But for the most part, no.

Rarely single in my life, I certainly had never been single in swiping society. I had never dated before, only had relationships. I did not know how this game was played. I didn't want to play games anyway. I just wanted to be straightforward, direct me.

I kept my profile on Tinder short. It started out as:

Looking for arm candy + love.

I thought that was clear. It didn't work.
I eventually changed it. I tried:

I have a lot of stamina. Can you keep up with me?

This of course was a double entendre. I really do have a lot of stamina. In general. This profile taught me that men in DC are not very clever. And that they have one track minds. It was a bore.
I went more direct:

Looking for someone to literally charm my pants off.

I just really wanted some charm in my life. That one taught

me that charm is in even shorter supply in DC than I had realized and reaffirmed that men have one track minds, as they only focused on the pants part and not on the charm part. At all. I was so unimpressed.

Since guys were always asking to take me out for a drink and I am not into drinking, I offered in my profile:

Let's go for a walk and get ice cream.

I didn't get a boyfriend, but at least I was treated to a few ice cream cones!

I cared about how my profile and photos appeared but as I swiped, I kept seeing the same things over and over. Here are some thoughts I compiled as I swiped:

- I don't care if you are new to DC.
- I don't care what your pet looks like.
- That is great that you can scuba dive but it doesn't show your FACE.
- I don't care if you are new to Tinder/Bumble.
- I don't care that you have a picture of you with someone famous.
- Why are you making me turn my phone sideways to look at your pictures? Do you not know how to "rotate?!"
- I really don't care about the size of the fish you caught.
- Wow, that is a pretty sunset. But who cares? It doesn't show your FACE.
- I love skiing too but I can't see your FACE behind the goggles.
- Lucky you to have so many friends but which one are YOU?
- I really do not want to see pictures of you posing with girls who are hotter than me. Hello!

- You want a partner in crime? Jail isn't my thing.
- Oh, you love to laugh? Me too. DUH.

Was this really what I had to choose from? Bad photos, bad marketing, bad profile descriptions? Left. Left. Left. It was so depressing. I swiped left so much I thought I was going to get carpal tunnel.

That was what attracted me to Nathan at first. Not only was he extremely attractive but his photos were good, quality photos. Clearly he cared about how he represented himself and aesthetics. I felt like I wouldn't have anything in common with someone who didn't. I also wondered, if they put so little effort into their profile, how much effort would they put into actually dating? My own pictures were carefully curated. I selected flattering photos that were both up to date *and* good quality. If I met someone, I didn't want him to be immediately disappointed because my pictures were not a good representation of me. On a few occasions I found myself on dates with guys whose pictures were clearly ten years old. That was false advertising and it seriously annoyed me.

I mostly swiped left.

After almost two years of Tinder and Bumble, I have had countless matches and conversations with guys, either just on the apps or in person. I have gone on first dates with over one hundred guys. My conversion rate to second date is 26%. Conversion rate to third date is 8%. Out of 100+ men, there was a mutual interest in going out a fourth time only 5% of the time. That is *not* a great statistic. Conversion rate to twelve dates: one. Nathan. Conversion rate to boyfriend? 0%.

Through messaging with these App Guys and meeting them in person, I learned a lot:

- Every guy thinks he has a "big/fat/thick/hard cock," no matter how small it is.

- Bad manners run rampant.
- Confusion is way worse than rejection.
- Guys are shameless about sending bad quality photos in which they look terrible.
- Guys are shameless in general.
- Small talk is so easy to avoid if you actually just offer a few sentences about what you are up to.
- Nothing is taboo.
- Most guys have zero fear of STDs. They will try to have sex with you without a condom and without asking if you have been tested, or if you are even on birth control.
- If you can't handle being ignored, cancelled on, or blown off, don't even consider putting yourself out there.
- Many guys ask for pictures and the more you show, the more they want to see. They say "please" when they ask for them.
- If you oblige requests for naked photos, they will almost certainly *not* meet you in person, no matter how hot you are.
- Young guys LOVE the idea of being with an older woman.
- No one should take rejection personally because no one controls feeling a spark.
- Charm is in rare supply.
- The best time to swipe and engage in conversation is on Saturday mornings because guys are in bed and horny.
- Perfect strangers will ask you sexual questions *way* before you expect it.
- Dick pics should be solicited.
- Guys will kiss you way too soon, often before even paying you a single compliment and definitely without asking permission.
- Many guys just want to get you naked as fast as possible

and many are only concerned with their own pleasure and put in no effort whatsoever into making sure you are satisfied.

- A good distraction from a hot 27 year old not paying attention to you is getting banged by a hot 23 year old (specifically, a muscular, blonde one who looks like an Abercrombie model).

You *can* have fun sometimes with these dating apps though too. In the beginning, before I learned all these lessons and heard the same things over and over, to the point of getting sick of it, I did have fun. I liked and needed the attention. In most cases, the guys were nice. Sometimes you could get into really open and honest discussions. Some of the best conversations I had were with people who I never actually ended up meeting. Maybe they were shy to know me in real life after divulging so many of their most secret thoughts to me? I did make a few friends on the apps who I have never met but feel like I know. Maybe it is better that we never met because I didn't really keep any friends from the ones I did meet in person. Except Nathan.

Sometimes on these apps you can be funny and you can be clever. Out of the blue, one day in wintertime, a man who I had only exchanged one message with told me, "I'd love to roll around in the hay with you." I told him I thought it was the wrong season for hay.

One time a guy asked me, right at the very beginning of our conversation, to send him "an ass pic." I took a screenshot of his profile pic and sent it to him.

Yeah, sometimes you can have fun. But it gets old. The first time someone told me

You're stunning.
Will you sit on my face?

I was shocked. I couldn't believe someone would just say something like that to me just like that. But, I didn't want to get worked up and upset about it. So, I just told him:

> I don't know whether to lecture you or take you
> up on your offer.

We actually had a few days of fun and inappropriate conversation after that, until he ghosted. He was the first one who ghosted on me, the first of many. I don't know why he did it. I don't know why people ghost, period. I do know that it is an unkind, cowardly and lazy tactic. I knew that ghosting was a thing when I met Nathan and I lived in fear that he would do that to me. It was scary liking someone new after being in a relationship for six years. I was terrified of being ignored. I wasn't afraid because of how much I loved him, I was afraid because I just hate being treated with bad manners. Luckily, Nathan never did that to me. But, I have been ignored by many others since him. I am probably being actively ignored by at least five men at the moment.

12 *Constant Rejection*

I have been ghosted on, ignored, cancelled on at the last minute, cancelled on by being unmatched, and rejected constantly. My phone often feels like it is just a rejection apparatus. I walk around carrying this cruel device, being rejected constantly on multiple platforms by multiple people. Rejected on Bumble, Tinder, Facebook messenger, SMS, Whatsapp, Google Hangouts. I am rejected by people I am interested in and by people in whom I am not interested. Constant, constant rejection.

I am now a pro at rejection. I am a pro at both giving and receiving rejection. Some of my skill I learned from Nathan. His rejection was direct, honest, straightforward and clear. He was my rejection mentor. When I need to provide some rejection of my own, I think WWND? He made it seem effortless. These are skills everyone should have. Take rejection with grace; thank them for their honesty and wish them well. Give rejection with clarity. Don't confuse people.

Confusion is actually so much worse than rejection. If someone rejects you, you know you have to move on. But when someone confuses you? You feel insecure, you question every move you make, you become "crazy." *Why hasn't he responded? Should I text him again or not? Is he ignoring me or dead in a ditch somewhere?* These are questions no one should ever be put in the position of having to ask themselves. It just isn't nice and it isn't necessary. If someone confuses me, I call him out on it. One line I like to use is "Are we ignoring each other now? :)" That allows him to clarify without being accusatory. And, I will definitely get my answer whether or not one is provided. People who confuse people are just mean. It is very easy to just tell someone "I don't feel the connection that I want to feel in order to pursue something." Chemistry is not personal and stating its lack is not unkind. It is best to be honest and clear about it. No one needs to get offended or have their feelings hurt because no one controls when that spark or that connection happens. It just does or it doesn't. It is not a choice.

13 Naked Selfies and Not Boyfriends (the Prop Roster)

In the beginning of my Tinder/Bumble experience, I went on tons of dates. Some weeks I had dates almost every night. Though I tried to mix it up and go out with men who were age appropriate, I found few to swipe right on. I tried; I really did. But, it got depressing. With so many matches with guys in their twenties, I thought "Why not?" I needed some excitement. Dating guys in their twenties was so much more fun and very good for the ego. I liked their good looks and their energy, their bodies that they hadn't let go. I liked being desired by them. I liked that they still had their lifetimes ahead of them and hadn't amassed failures and baggage to be negative about, but especially I liked that they were open and not set in their ways and spouting off lists of resentful deal breakers. I felt on their wavelength because, despite being older and having failures of my own, I felt young on the inside and luckily, still looked young on the outside. I wondered how they saw me when they were with me. Was I that "older woman" or an energetic and fun peer? Mostly I just ached to distract myself from thinking about Nathan, so I used them as they used me, my mantra at the time being "Why have one boyfriend when I can have a different boyfriend every night of the week?"

I mean, what do you do when you are in your forties, you look like you are in your early thirties, and you are a sexual being who feels like her body is going to waste and is having *constant* anxiety about aging?

The first thing you do is take a lot of naked selfies.

I wish that I had started taking naked selfies when I was in my twenties, or even in high school. I take them for myself, to have when I am older so I can look back at the beautiful, proportional body with which I was blessed.

When I started taking them, it wasn't with the purpose of sending them to App Guys. These strangers just ended up being the lucky recipients of the evidence of my vanity/conceit/narcissism/photography skills. I was very generous with these photos because I was proud of them and I loved the reaction they got. I needed male attention; without it, I felt like my insides were withering and dying. I learned that sending photos procured me enough attention to minimally satisfy that need through the compliments I received. In the beginning, hearing how hot I was and how sexy I was and how amazing my body was served as an exciting supplement for what I did not have, someone to prevent me from feeling like I was always alone in the backseat.

I didn't have what I wanted, that one person, that lifetime partner. I had the opposite - scores of strangers who couldn't have cared less about me. Although the opposite of what I would have wanted, I am still grateful to those strangers for their compliments and attention, as they were better than nothing.

The second thing you do is get a Roster.

Since I had always been in relationships it caused me a lot of stress and anxiety to not have someone to be intimate with regularly. That was not something I was used to and not something I was willing to accept, despite being single. I didn't want a list of sexual partners that was ten miles long either, so I thought that if I could get repeats, maybe I could satisfy my needs without getting too high a number. I needed a Roster. A Roster of Not Boyfriends so I could hopefully have that intimate human contact at least once a week (how was this my life that it was so infrequent?!). Most people refer to Not Boyfriends as "friends with benefits" but given that I am particular about language, I do not like that term. These guys were not my friends. They didn't care about me or check in with me like a friend would. That is a shame, but that is how it was.

I worked hard to develop my Roster. Sometimes it worked and sometimes it didn't. Some weeks I would have to solicit every Not Boyfriend I had and still get nothing. That was so depressing and anxiety producing. I couldn't believe how hard it was to get someone to have sex with me. It made no sense. What were these guys doing that sex was so low on their list of priorities? I was fun, laidback, easygoing, not trying to tie them down, my body was smoking, yet I could barely get their attention. Occasionally, there were some weeks that I didn't have to solicit anyone and I would get to be in the position of turning people down because

I had more solicitations than I had time to accommodate. That was rare but a much better scenario since I felt like I was in a constant race against the clock, that I was aging by the minute. I felt so much pressure and anxiety over taking advantage of my body while I still looked youthful and desirable. It was not a good feeling. It is still not a good feeling.

With Nathan I had discovered how much better intimacy is with a mirror. He was so incredible looking that I wanted to be able to see him, watch him. But, I couldn't believe how amazing my own body looked. It was beautiful. I wanted to see that over and over again, which caused me more anxiety because I didn't have someone with whom I could see myself regularly. My Not Boyfriends became my props so I could watch *myself.* They didn't seem to mind.

I don't get why we think of sex as "bad" and "dirty" and "naughty." It is a beautiful and amazing and I think it should be revered as such. And if you get to do that with someone you love who loves you back? You are the luckiest. And you should not take it for granted. *Ever.* I haven't had that in a long time.

14 Nate

Nate is one of my Not Boyfriends. He is a very good prop. He was 24 when we went on our first date. He was so adorable with his cute face and buzz cut and light blue eyes. If I had been younger, I would have absolutely wanted to date his adorable self and help him shop for clothes that fit properly. We went to P.F. Chang's in my neighborhood. Nate seemed genuinely interested in getting to know me, which was nice. He was likeable. But, given our age difference, there was clearly no future despite whatever sparks were flying. It was pointless to pretend otherwise. Nate came home with me. His stamina did not disappoint and we have seen each other many times since.

But, when I realized what we had done that first time, I couldn't stop laughing.

Do you know what that was? P.F. Chang's + sex?

Yes, that is right...

We Chang'd and banged.

Hahahahaha!

15 Rolex Alex

Alex I actually met in real life, not on a dating app. I was out one night with some friends in the bar at the Four Seasons and when he walked in we caught each other's eye and he maintained his gaze. That was nice - I had not been looked at like that in a while, not since Danny in London. After a bit, Alex came over to our table and asked if he could join us which caused my pulse to quicken and my hopefulness to spring into action. He was handsome, a clone of a young Gerard Butler. My friends got up from our table and went to the bar so Alex and I could talk. His British accent charmed me, though his drunken state did not. I kept having to dodge incoming kisses that did not interest me from a total and drunken stranger. It was hard to keep up a conversation with someone who could barely speak coherently. But, he was attractive and well dressed and I sensed that his sober self would be someone enjoyable to know. We exchanged numbers. I texted him right then and there and told him to text me when he was sober. Then, all of a sudden, for some reason, he took off his watch and put it on my wrist. I don't know what prompted him to do that. As he did it, I looked down and saw that the watch was a Rolex.

Hmmm.

A Rolex? On my wrist. A Rolex on my wrist from a guy who was probably too drunk to remember that he even put it there.

Hmmm.

"Please please please let him forget that he did that," I thought to myself. "Please let him be too drunk to remember what he did." My plan? Walk out of there with the Rolex and either definitely be assured an actual date with a sober version of this handsome Brit, or, if he blew me off, definitely make a few thousand dollars, compensation from him on behalf of himself and every other guy who had blown me off in the past year. Had I become bitter? Maybe a little. Cynical? Sadly, definitely.

When my friends came back to the table and told me they were ready to leave, I practically jumped out of my seat. Rolex still in place, I said a quick goodbye to Alex and was out the door. I was giddy from my exploit. My friends were scandalized. We waited for the Uber as I kept looking back, hoping he would not come out the door to claim what was his. He did not.

The next day Alex texted me and asked me out on a proper date for later that week. And by the way, did I have any idea what happened to his watch? "Yep, it is on my nightstand."

It was nice to have that collateral. That was the first date I went on in over a year with zero percent anxiety that the guy would actually show up. As suspected, sober Alex was pleasant and I enjoyed his company. After our date, before I even got a block away, he texted me that he was "very glad we met." I liked that very much. And yes, he did get his watch back.

Alex and I had a second date the following week. And then I didn't hear from him for a while. I am so used to this by now that it doesn't even faze me anymore. More time passed and I figured I probably would never hear from him again. But then out of the blue, he invited me over for dinner a few weeks ago. I was happy to take him up on his offer as spontaneous invitations are my favorite and I needed some male attention. I arrived at his very nice apartment, that had actual grown up furniture and a nice masculine style, to find a charcuterie selection on the coffee table, the dinner table set, and a whole chicken roasting in the oven. Well, that was pleasant! We had a nice time, the food and presentation were lovely and I liked the way he smelled and listening to his accent.

I think we might still be seeing each other, but honestly, I have no idea. He barely texts me and if I text him, he takes forever to respond, if he even responds at all. I think we are doing something in two weeks. But who knows? I may never even see him again. It's pretty lame. But that is how dating is today: lame.

When I first started dating Nathan, I didn't know that this was how dating worked as I had only had relationships before. When I know what I want, I am not afraid to go after it so I was not very shy about asking him to schedule the next and the next and the next date. I must have come across as very intense to his more reserved self. I also messaged him a lot, wanting to get to know him and wanting him to get to know me. I loved messaging with him. He was always brief but his choice of words was always so funny and clever and on point. I had so much chemistry with his words. I swooned at everything he said, especially if it was something flirty or complimentary. I admired him for his cleverness. He brought out the funniest, most clever version of myself and I liked that too. Because I didn't want to overwhelm him with messages, *not* messaging him became a full-time job. I wanted to message him constantly so it was a lot of work not to! A *lot*. It often still feels like a full-time job. Sometimes I wonder if I had been less intense and just proceeded more slowly if I could have seen him longer, before he decided our age difference was a deal breaker. I wonder if I could have spaced it out over more time, maybe he would have gotten attached, as our fondness was not one-sided. But what is the point even of wondering these things? I have to remind myself to just be grateful to have the happy memories I do have with him and to know that I have no regrets about ever holding anything back.

16 *Best Birthday Present Everr*

Before Alex there was another Brit. Danny. I met Danny on the street in London. When I walk down the street in DC, I feel invisible. Men rarely acknowledge me. They don't even look at me. I am not one of those women who gets offended by a stranger telling me to smile. I would welcome it! Maybe because it rarely happens to me? But also because the energy you expend at getting mad from someone telling you to smile is way more effort than actually smiling. And smiling is good for you and good for the world. I do not understand these people who choose to get upset about smiling rather than just do it.

Anyway, I was in London with my best friend Kim and her daughter Kayley. We had just come back from seeing the musical *Matilda*. I hated it. I slept through half of it. I was full of negative energy from sitting through that torture and, at ten o'clock at night in London, definitely not in the mood to go to bed. And then there we were, one block from the apartment we had rented and crossing paths with Danny, his gaze fixated on me, such a welcome, refreshing gaze after feeling invisible for months (years?). We smiled and kept walking. Kim and Kayley kept looking back and telling me, "He is still looking at you!" We got to our building and I looked back and sure enough, there he was, just milling about, still looking at me. "Well, if he is going to keep staring at me, we might as well go and introduce ourselves," I said as I herded us back in his direction. "Hi! I am Jennifer. This is Kim and Kayley." Introductions were made, pleasantries were exchanged. And then flat out, "Do you have a boyfriend?" *Ha.* "Nope. I sure do not. But I could use a British boyfriend for the night!" He liked the idea and asked if I wanted to go a pub.

Um, heck YEAH!

You just never know *what* can happen. Right when the last thing that I wanted to do was go home and go to bed, my orbit crossed with this handsome, bearded and blue-eyed Englishman. I couldn't believe how lucky I was. I went back to the apartment quickly to brush my teeth and freshen up, as we had been out all day, and then I flew back down the stairs hoping that he hadn't run away. Sure enough, he was still there waiting for me! Given that it had already been established that we were going to be boyfriend and girlfriend for the night, when he planted one on me, right there and then, I loved it! Having removed all boundaries between us, he took my hand and held it just like a boyfriend should as led me to the pub where his friends were. The sparks were flying, the energy between us was intense. We were both all in, knowing that we only had one night to enjoy each other. In my experience, those are the most fun love affairs. Relationships where both people know that they have limited time together allows the men to be open, affectionate, loving, and boundary free - like my 24-hour-ski-instructor-boyfriend Alessandro in Italy a few years back, one of the best "relationships" of my life!

Danny and I could not get enough of each other. As our conversation easily flowed, he charmed me by keeping track of all the things we had in common. We were unafraid to look into each other's eyes, to flirt, to enjoy. I wanted to get out of the pub; it was too noisy to talk comfortably. I wanted to walk around the city with him and hold hands and make out on street corners, and that ended up being exactly what we did. In a secluded spot, his hand was down my pants, his finger inside me. On the street. In London. He was bold. But it felt right - he was my boyfriend, after all. I couldn't not take him home with me. We quietly snuck into my room and enjoyed each other all night. I was so high off his vibe that I could barely sleep. In the morning when he kissed me goodbye, I felt so grateful that I got to share that amazing moment with him. But, after he left, the sadness crept in as I questioned why I could never find that in DC - that spark, that connection, that excitement, that unabashed blissing out on each other. It was so frustrating!

It was clear that Danny was younger but we did not discuss our ages. He was actually the one who said we could just "not go there." That was fine with me because I needed a break from being 42 and single that night. I just wanted to be an American girl in London with a handsome stranger. I was curious how old he was though. I figured young twenties, maybe 25? Months later, on my birthday, I messaged him and asked, since we were probably never going to see each other again, would he satisfy my curiosity? He did.

He was nineteen.

I can't think of a better birthday present for a single 43 year old!

17 I learned to ski in Italy.

The best decision I ever made in my life was when I was 23 years old and said yes to Caterina. I had already been an au pair in France and was living in Argentina teaching English at the time and I didn't want to start life in the real world yet. I wanted to continue living abroad and practicing the languages I had studied. I was already fluent in Spanish and French and I wanted to work on my Italian.

When I applied to be an au pair in Italy, I requested to not be placed in a family with children under the age of six. I did not want to burden myself with diapers or potty training and I did not want to deal with a pre-verbal child. That would neither be fun for me, nor beneficial for my Italian fluency. The agency put me in contact with a woman named Caterina who was very interested in me. She had four daughters…

All under the age of six.

No thank you.

But, Caterina wouldn't take no for an answer. She offered to pay for my plane ticket, to pay for me to study Italian, to take me skiing *and* she had a housekeeper.

Well, twist my arm.

This was an offer I could not refuse.

This was before the internet was a blip on anyone's radar so googling Venice, where Caterina's family lived, was not on my agenda. Google did not even exist yet! I had never seen any pictures of Venice so I had no idea whatsoever that Venice was a city built in the water, water that was a beautiful greenish blue like the Mediterranean. I had no idea until I actually got there that the next four months of my life were going to be carless, that I would be wandering my way on foot around that maze of a centuries-old city being dazzled by the Byzantine and Moorish architecture and that I would be living in an apartment in a palazzo right on the Grand Canal near the Rialto Bridge. What a wonderful surprise that all was! I think it was the biggest surprise of my life and maybe the reason that when I plan vacations I don't like to have an agenda - I just focus on the logistics and don't look things up ahead of time. TripAdvisor is not a resource that I use. Ever. I want to be surprised, to see what I see and to, maybe, capture that complete and utter newness one more time. Although, few places can compare to the uniqueness of Venice because Venice is not just a place; Venice is an experience.

Many people I talk to who have travelled to Italy say that Venice is their least favorite. They prefer Rome and Florence. I can't imagine feeling that way but I think that it is because vacationing in Venice is different from actually *living* in Venice. Staying in a hotel and eating in restaurants is not the same as living on the Grand Canal and eating homemade meals cooked by Caterina and Signora Olesia, the glamorous housekeeper who looked more like she belonged shopping on 5th Avenue than making gnocchi in Caterina's kitchen. Knowing which greengrocer sells the freshest produce at the best price, shopping at the fish market on Saturdays, taking four little girls all dressed in matching outfits by boat to school was *living* in Venice. That is different from visiting Venice.

Four girls. Marta was five, Anna Chiara was three, Bianca and Claudia were two year old twins. It actually didn't matter that they were all under six because they were indeed potty trained and verbal. They all slept in the same big room together, four little beds all lined up in a row. In the mornings Caterina and I would wake them up and get them dressed and ready for school, a time-consuming task because everything had to be done in multiples of four. Each morning was a race against the clock to catch the Venetian version of the school bus, the vaporetto. Their apartment was on the top floor of the palazzo and every morning we would have to run down the 91 stairs as fast as we could to catch the boat, Caterina with Anna Chiara on one hip and one of the twins on the other, me with a twin on my hip, and little Marta scurrying down ahead. It is a miracle we never fell down the stairs!

After school it was the opposite; it would take *forever* to get those tired little girls back up the 91 stairs. Back in the apartment, they first would sit on their potties, all lined up in the bathroom looking at books and doing little puzzles, before scampering off to the playroom until dinnertime. From the playroom window you could look out on the terracotta rooftops of Venice, hear the ringing of church bells and on very clear days you could see all the way to the Italian Alps, far off in the distance. Four busy little bees buzzing around that room, playing dress up, coloring, Marta leading games of make believe, more coloring, fighting over the black marker. Claudia was very possessive of that black marker. Anyone else who tried to use it risked ending up with bloody scratches. I don't know why it never occurred to us to get more black markers!

There were many fun moments and memories from living in Venice - walking the girls to school in the morning, helping them learn to dress themselves, sitting in the sun-filling kitchen talking with Signora Olesia as she bustled about preparing her delicious meals, learning the words to all sorts of children's songs in Italian and singing them with the girls. There was one activity, however, that was not fun: birthday parties.

Always an aficionado of interior decor, the bright side of having to go to these parties was that I loved getting to see the inside of beautiful Venetian homes when I had to accompany the girls to birthdays, but the miserable downside was that the hostesses were *not* friendly. They seemed to look down on me as if I were just the hired help, not a college-educated American there for a cultural exchange and to work on her Italian fluency - not that that should matter. Hired help or not, no one should be made to feel looked down upon. They were not warm and inclusive like Caterina. No one would talk to me at those parties. I would just sit by myself, being made to feel like the outsider that I was, and count down the minutes till I could go back to Caterina's welcoming home. I don't think I was dispositioned to ever be that way but I learned from those posh Venetian mothers' negative example exactly how *not* to make someone feel.

Thank goodness for Anna Chiara; she always provided comic relief at these unpleasant events. Whenever I had to accompany three year old Anna Chiara to one of those awful parties, she always wanted to see the bathroom. "Che pulito questo bagno!" *What a clean bathroom!* She would exclaim if it met her expectations. I don't know why Anna was always on bathroom inspection duty, but she was. When she visited me in the States later, all grown up, I was nervous for my bathroom to pass her inspection.

I spoke English to the girls and they spoke Italian to me. As time passed, they started to pick up some English words and understood certain phrases (Time to brush your teeth! Time for bed! Finish your soup. Stop it. Hurry up. Come on.) but they didn't have much of a grasp on grammar. After school when they had been on their potties for what seemed like long enough, I would ask them, "Are you done?" And they would respond to me, "Are you done." I would laugh and say, "No, are *you* done?" And they would respond, "Are *you* done." It was so cute!

In the beginning they were so spoiled they did not even know how to ask for a glass of water without crying. I did not allow that. I made them stand in the corner until they stopped. They spent a lot of time in that corner. But, they learned to stop crying. The twins were very attached to their previous nanny and to Signora Olesia. They wanted nothing to do with me in the beginning. "Non ti voglio!" That was what they said to me when I would try to get near them. *I don't want you!* But, by the end of my time with them, despite my strict rules and all the time they had to spend standing in the corner, they were fighting over who got to sit on my lap every night before bed while we watched the "Doe a deer" scene from *The Sound of Music.* I loved them so much and they loved me back.

As Caterina had promised, we did go skiing. However, we weren't a family going on a ski trip: we were an entourage, first travelling by boat and then needing three cars to transport ten of us, the family of six plus the "staff" - Signora Olesia and her husband, Caterina's childhood nanny, their au pair (me), plus

25 pieces of luggage! I never saw anyone pack like Caterina. She brought every single thing that they could possibly need, including the entire contents of her medicine cabinet, as if there were no stores or pharmacies where we were headed. Her philosophy was that although overstuffed suitcases may be a pain when you are in transit, they are worth it in order to avoid the regret of wishing for something you had left behind while you are at your destination. I used to pride myself on my ability to pack lightly, but, in this and many other ways, Caterina influenced me. Now I don't stress about over packing. What? Ten pairs of shoes is too much for one week? If they fit in the suitcase, who cares?

Despite having grown up in Maine, I did not learn to ski as a child. Caterina taught me to ski as an adult, an American girl in Cortina d'Ampezzo, au pair to a Venetian family, observing the rich Romans, Venetians, and Milanese skiing down the mountains in their fur lined jackets, usually with a cell phone to their ear and a scowl on their face as their nannies attended to their children. I didn't know what they had to be so unhappy about. They were in one of the most exclusive places in the world and they were beautiful and rich. Yet, they looked miserable. I, however, was not miserable. I was thrilled to be there. I was thrilled to be learning a new skill, thrilled to have lunch with Caterina and her husband Giulio at one of the mountaintop restaurants where you could only eat if you were able to ski there, thrilled to be in the Dolomite Mountains for the first time. How can you possibly be unhappy while you are eating a prosciutto and butter panino with the winter sun beating down on your face and the bright blue, cloudless sky contrasting with the white snow-covered mountains as you breathe in the fresh winter air and listen to Italian spoken all around you?

Joining Caterina's family was the best decision of my life for so many reasons. I learned a new skill - I finally had a sport. I did not participate in sports growing up so having an athletic ability made me feel confident and proud. To this day, I still cannot believe that I have an athletic skill, that I can ski and ski fast and well. I became fluent in Italian. I learned to cook pasta perfectly al dente and can impress friends with my risotto. I learned all sorts of delicious recipes - zuppa di pesce, ditalini with garbanzos, orecchiette with broccoli, penne with zucchini. I still have so many recipes to learn from Caterina - her meatballs and her stuffed tomatoes are to die for. I have gotten to go back to Venice multiple times and always have a free place to stay. I learned to love the mountains and have taken amazing ski vacations in France and in Italy, witnessing some of the most beautiful views in the world, which I never would have seen if not for saying yes to Caterina. But most importantly of all, I made lifelong friends. Caterina and I have been friends now for twenty years. I feel so lucky that despite not having children of my own, I got to have a little glimpse into what it feels like to love four little girls with all my heart, that I got to have them fight over who got to sit on my lap, and that I got to watch them grow up into beautiful, smart, funny, cool young women who I have known for almost their whole lives.

18 Best Relationship Ever

Today my little Venetian girls are all beautiful young ladies who have graduated from college and are now my friends. A few years ago I visited Marta in Cortina where she was becoming a ski instructor. Though grown up, Marta was still the same sweet, kind, considerate, patient soul I had met when she was five. I just adore her. She was such a good hostess, taking me skiing every day, giving me pointers to help me improve my speed and confidence, showing me the best mountaintop restaurants, cooking pasta with radicchio for me - ensuring that I learned yet another recipe to add to my repertoire. I was so happy to be with her and so grateful to my 23 year old self for making a decision that enabled our orbits to cross paths.

One night, we went out with her friends and I met Alessandro. I didn't pay him much attention and just enjoyed being out, surrounded by handsome ski instructors, listening to everyone speak Italian, not believing that this was actually my life. A few nights later Marta arranged for us to have dinner with Alessandro and Massimo, her boyfriend at the time. I was ambivalent about Alessandro and was just looking forward to going out for pizza, in Cortina, in Italy, with my dear Italian friend and getting to practice my Italian. But, when we arrived and met in front of the restaurant and I saw the confident, flirtatious Alessandro in his very cool Italian jacket, I suddenly became his in an instant. I am a sucker for a well-dressed flirt.

We sat down at our table, Alessandro and I across from Marta and Massimo. Within minutes (seconds?) Alessandro was holding my hand under the table. I loved it. I loved his bold charm, his unabashed claim on what he wanted to be his. A natural flirt myself, I announced to them all, "I am going home with him tonight." I spent the night with Alessandro and I felt like I was living a dream. American woman in Italy having a love affair with an Italian ski instructor? Was this my life?!

Alessandro was my first 24-hour boyfriend. I had never been one for one night stands, so I thought if I framed it as if we were boyfriend and girlfriend, it would be okay to be intimate since we were in a "relationship." When I proposed to Alessandro that he be my boyfriend for the 24 hours we had together, until he had to leave to go to his family's for the weekend, he eagerly jumped right into the role. I spent the night in his arms, enjoying his muscular body and unforgettably soft skin, whispering with him in Italian as we savored each other. In the morning, he treated me to breakfast on the mountain before we spent the day skiing together. After each run we rode the lift together, kissing and taking off our gloves so we could hold hands. He introduced me to all his friends we ran into on the slopes as if I really were his girlfriend. Alessandro, my 24-hour-Italian-ski-instructor boyfriend - best relationship ever! I always smile and feel so lucky when I think of that nice memory.

At the end of the day when he had to leave, Marta and Massimo picked me up to go back to Marta's. And there I was once again, alone in the backseat.

19 Future in-laws / Former in-laws

Getting divorced was the hardest thing I ever had to do. Though I spent most of my marriage unhappy and wanting a divorce, or thinking I wanted one, it wasn't until Alejandro closed the door that I realized I hadn't wanted a divorce at all. I just wanted him to give me what I didn't know how to get from him. I was heartbroken. I missed him terribly. We had been together for twelve years. We met when I was 23 and he was 22.

We became adults together, the blind leading the blind, neither of us knowing how to be adults, get along, communicate, deal with a cross-cultural divide, him living in the United States for me, missing his family, friends, lifestyle and culture in Argentina.

After my time as an au pair in Italy, I went back to Argentina to visit him. We were still very much in love and had done "long distance" while I was in Venice. This was at the beginning of email, so technology made our relationship possible. It was before free international calling, Skype, Whatsapp or any of those things would have made it *easy*. I remember Caterina had a cell phone that she would sometimes lend me and I would walk around Venice pretending to talk to Alejandro on the phone, entertaining myself with imaginary conversations that allowed me to express my love to the universe, if not to him directly.

I had planned to stay in Argentina for three weeks and then go back to the States to finally get a real job and start life as an adult. At that time, Alejandro was very attached to me and he did not want me to leave. Every day he reminded me how few days I had left. I didn't want to leave him either. So, we decided to see if I could start teaching English privately and amass enough students to make a reasonable income. We made flyers and put them up all over Santa Fe, the city where he lived. At that time, I felt like we were a team - we were on a mission together. And, people started calling! We did it! I started my own business of teaching English privately and I was able to stay - three weeks turned into a year.

In addition, I also got a job teaching American culture at an English institute. One day, I told my students the story of how I had ended up in Argentina teaching them - how my three week vacation to visit Alejandro was a last minute plan I had made while at the time it was summer where I was living and therefore, I had only been able to pack summer clothes despite the fact that I was headed to winter in Argentina. Since I was on a very tight budget, I couldn't shop for new clothes. As I told my class, "I only have three pairs of socks here." I pointed to my socks and showed them, "These are Alejandro's socks. This is Alejandro's sweater. I am embarrassed all the time by how I am dressed because in Santa Fe all the girls are so stylish and every day I have to wear the same thing. But, the embarrassment is worth it because I get to be with Alejandro." We really were in love back then. I sacrificed fashion for him!

In order to save money on bus fare I bought a bike. I rode that yellow bike all over Santa Fe to my students' houses. I was the only person in that whole city who wore a helmet, not even the motorcyclists wore helmets. I stood out like a sore thumb, but I didn't care. Since I am an only child, my parents have no back up. I have to be careful!

Alejandro's parents Juan and Mari welcomed me into their home with warmth and generosity. In Santa Fe everyone goes home for lunch so we sat around the table together every day for both our afternoon and evening meals. Juan was a jokester, always in a good mood, never serious. This frustrated the family at times. They were always exasperatedly yelling "Papá!!" But I loved his laid back ways and I knew that if you told him you needed to speak to him seriously, he would oblige you. Mari worked full time but still bustled around the house when she was home, taking pride in accomplishing the household duties, performing them with the gravitas of a matriarch, showering us with love, spoiling us. Alejandro's younger sister Minia and I became close friends and confidants. She was the one who taught me how to iron my hair (life changing!!) and to spend more time and effort primping. I loved the way she dressed and she became my biggest fashion influence. Minia with the light brown eyes and blonde hair, so naturally pretty that she is one of the few people who actually looks *worse* with makeup. Minia with the bangle bracelets that clinked when she walked so Alejandro and I had fair warning that she was approaching if we were sneaking a moment of intimacy;

thank goodness for those bracelets because Minia had the habit of *not* knocking.

On Sundays Juan would cook asados (Argentine barbecue) for us, in the asador (a kind of open oven) that was up on the roof of the house because they didn't have a yard. Juan made the BEST asados. I was so lucky that I got to eat authentic Argentine asados on a weekly basis! While he worked on the meats, Mari prepared the accompanying salads. We didn't do much to help at all, the parents taking care of us. I feel so grateful to have shared those amazing meals, oftentimes with friends or family joining because there was always room for more around Juan and Mari's table. The best part though was later, after siesta, when it was too hot to do anything and we would just sit around lethargic, and someone would say, "Pedimos helado?" *Shall we order some ice cream?* And everyone would start shouting out the flavors they wanted and we would call La Americana and put in our order and then listen for the sound of the motorcycle that would arrive soon after with our ice cream delivery. God, I loved that.

I had my own room in Juan and Mari's house but my room did not have air conditioning. Summers are extremely hot and humid in Santa Fe, and in their house the only bedroom with an air conditioning unit was theirs. Sleeping in my own room would have been unbearable - it was too sweltering. On those oppressively hot nights, we would all sleep together in Juan and Mari's room. Minia in the bed with her parents and Alejandro and I on either side of the bed on the floor. You can't get much closer than that. Those were happy times. My three week vacation had turned into a year of living with my future in-laws, until I finally really did have to go back to the States and start my grown-up life.

I loved them. I was part of the family. It was so nice to really, actually be a part of the family that I married into, to *really* know them. After Alejandro and I were married, Juan and Mari would come to visit us in the States, long visits because the airfare was so expensive. Sometimes they would stay for 45 days in our one bedroom apartment with us. It was never long enough. I have always loved family time and Alejandro was happier during those times so we didn't fight as much. I never wanted them to leave. We were very close and not having them be my in-laws anymore was one of the worst parts of divorcing. And, it wasn't just Alejandro's parents I lost as my in-laws in the divorce, but his sister and all the aunts and uncles and cousins I had gotten to know and loved. His cousin Maria Cruz? I had gone to her quinciañera. His little cousin Flopi who I had met when she was nine? I had seen her grow up! That was a very hard reality to accept, that all these people were no longer going to be my *family*. I had always wanted a big family and I had gotten that through Alejandro. And, it wasn't just that they were a big family - they were also a very nice and fun and close family who enjoyed each other's company and laughed together, who weren't just relatives but were actually best friends as well. The good news, at least, is that I believe that they were equally fond of me, so we are all still friends on Facebook and I have seen them on return solo trips to Argentina. Our fondness and relationship hasn't really changed, just the frequency of visits and the label. But ooof, losing that label? That was *really* hard to take.

20 Santa Fe, Argentina

Santa Fe, Argentina is where I acquired the two younger sisters I had always wanted but never had, where I became part of two more families, my original host family and my future husband's family and where I didn't learn the lessons I needed to learn there until after I didn't live there anymore.

Santa Fe is not a place I would call pretty, though it does have some very pretty vegetation. It is extremely flat, laid out in a grid of endless blocks. In most parts of the city there are just blocks and blocks of houses, all attached to each other. No side yards, no front yards, just houses right on the sidewalks with no space between neighbors. They aren't charming row houses, just plain little boxes. Sprinkled here and there are a few that are very old and rundown, adorned with beautiful beaux-arts details, relics of when Argentina was a very rich country. There are also, surprisingly to me, many that are deco in style. But, mostly they are just plain and unappealing.

Santa Fe is on the Paraná river, the second largest river in South America. But the Paraná is not pretty either. It is brown. I had never seen a brown river before because the rivers in Maine are blue. I appallingly thought it must be very polluted but was relieved to learn later that it was just brown from the sediment.

My first time in Santa Fe, I had come from Maine by way of the Côte d'Azure, so it was hard to live in a city that was not pleasing to the eye. I had grown up surrounded by beauty everywhere I looked and had just spent six months in the south of France. At least the people of Santa Fe were attractive - the Argentine girls seemed to all have perfect long, brown hair and perfect bodies. They were also experts at casual style, all clad in the tightest, low cut jeans that flattered them and showed off their perfect behinds. At least what I lacked in beauty from my surroundings, I had an abundance of to catch my eye from the people I met or passed on the street.

When I was introduced to people they would always ask me what I thought of Santa Fe. I didn't know what to say because I didn't want to hurt their feelings. I didn't want to tell them that I thought it was ugly. They were very, very proud of their city. They told me they missed it so much when they left. I did not understand why. Until one day, years later, I finally did.

In Santa Fe it seems like everyone knows each other. It isn't transient like in the States where you often grow up somewhere and then leave. In Argentina you usually stay put, or at least in Santa Fe you do. You grow up there with your same friends your whole life, your whole family often in the same neighborhood, walking distance. Santa Fe was about friends, about family, about relationships. I learned that this was what they missed when they were homesick for Santa Fe, as I myself eventually experienced that missing too. When you went downtown you would always run into people you knew. After spending time there, even I would run into people *I* knew. To be over 5,000 miles from home and to run into friends or acquaintances? That was a great feeling. It made me feel good to know people and to be known. It also reminded me of home where I too would always run into someone I knew when I was out and about.

Alejandro and I would go back every year at Christmastime. I was happy during those times at Christmas because I was surrounded by his family, instead of feeling like it was the most oppressively boring day of the year, as I had growing up, Jewish in Maine. We would go to his cousins' for Christmas Eve dinner, about twenty of us sitting around the table. The dinner wouldn't start till around ten at night; Argentines dine late. We would sit around that table for hours and hours and HOURS. Around 4 AM Alejandro would go out with his friends. Since I always preferred family time, I just stayed at the table. Was it till 6 AM? Seven? I don't remember anymore. We would finally go home to bed and then everyone would gather again at lunchtime, just a few hours later, for leftovers and more marathon sitting around the table.

I could not understand how these people, who knew each other their whole lives and saw each other all the time, still had so much to say to each other. There was so much laughing and storytelling. How did they still have new stories to tell? Eight hours around the table worth of stories? How? It boggled my mind.

When I first lived in Santa Fe it was very, very hard for me to participate in these gatherings. I did not have the patience to sit around a table for hours on end, late into the night. I was very uptight about going to bed early and getting up early. I had always been a morning person, influenced by Benjamin Franklin's mantra "early to bed, early to rise." I was the girl who was always looking at her watch, whose dream beach day was a day completely alone. Now I had to be surrounded by people all the time and often late into the night. Though I did like being surrounded by the people, the endless table sitting marathons and late hours were a huge culture clash for me and I never adjusted while I lived there.

However, each time I went back I slowly started to change. I began to see the value of just sitting and enjoying without an agenda. I stopped looking at my watch so much. I stopped being obsessed with going to bed early and getting up early. I started to be more flexible and to go with the flow and I learned that that was a way less stressful way to be! That was a very good lesson to learn and I am so grateful that my orbit crossed with Alejandro's so that I had the opportunity to learn it.

I never liked Santa Fe when I lived there, but every time I went back I started to like it more and more; it grew on me - not the city but the way of life - the long meals, the delicious asados, the afternoon siestas and the people. Sometimes I feel like I have more friends in that place on the other side of the world than I do right here at home. Between my former students and my former in-laws and my original host family, there is never enough time to see everyone when I go visit. Now when people ask me if I like Santa Fe, I don't have to be polite, I can just tell them, "Yes, yes I do" because I know now what that means.

21 Pionono Polenta, Pasta, and Pizza (or, Things You Learn in Santa Fe)

Though learning to just chill the f out was the most life-altering lesson I absorbed in Santa Fe, there are other things I learned that you learn when you live there:

You learn that atmospheric pressure makes you lethargic.

You learn that Argentines take their ice cream seriously and that there seems to be countless ice cream parlors. The ice cream itself is light but dense. It isn't overly creamy and tastes like it has way less calories than American ice cream. You hope that this is true because you eat a lot of it. You learn that one of the best ice cream shops in the whole world is La Americana, located on the corner of 25 de Mayo and Junín Streets, and that you can order ice cream over the phone and have it delivered.

You learn that they also happen to have the BEST pizza in Santa Fe, better than any pizza you ever had anywhere else in the world, even including in Italy.

You learn, despite your ethnocentric indoctrination, that there are entire sections of the world that couldn't care less about the United States because they have their own culture and their own politics and their own movies and their own fashion and their own TV shows and you learn that the U.S. is NOT actually the center of the universe.

You learn that asados are far superior to typical American backyard barbecues of hamburgers and hot dogs, that all the different meats from ribs to chinchulines (stuffed small intestines) to molleja (glands), to chorizo (sausage) and morcilla (blood sausage) are delicious and that molleja is your favorite. You learn that you love the accompanying carrot salad, salad of just shredded carrots and hardboiled egg, dressed with oil and vinegar but you never, ever learn the patience to shred those carrots yourself.

You learn that at Christmas they eat something called pionono and that it is the strangest food you have ever encountered: a cakey roll like the kind a jelly roll is made with but instead of jelly, it is stuffed with tuna fish and pineapple, iced with mayonnaise and topped with ham, decorated with pimento and olives. You never EVER learn to like this or the idea of this and you NEVER want to.

You learn that Argentines are mostly Caucasian because their origin is mostly Italian, German, or Spanish and that there are very few indigenous people in Argentina. You find it both incredibly interesting and sad that you can almost always infallibly tell someone's economic status by the color of their skin.

You learn that Argentines all hate their politicians no matter who is in office and that they all think that they are all corrupt, no matter the party affiliation. All politicians do is steal, according to the people you have talked to.

You learn how to make pasta from scratch and that there are no actual measurements - you just use "un huevo por persona." *One egg per serving.*

You learn that most families have domestic help and as you watch Carina ironing Alejandro's family's clothes, you learn how to iron perfectly, just like she does, and you remember her always when you iron shirts.

You learn that they feed their dogs polenta and even though you already never liked polenta, you learn to like it even less.

You learn that the men are very masculine but that they greet each other with kisses on the cheeks and sometimes hugs. You think that this is very sexy but a bit confusing. You wonder why these men in a more homophobic and machista culture are so much more comfortable being physically affectionate with each other than their American counterparts who are less homophobic but usually keep a much colder distance from their friends and relatives.

You learn that entire families can fit on a motorcycle and that this is a main method of transportation for many people.

You learn that the choripanes (chorizo in a bun) sold at the soccer stadium are a delicious delicacy and you learn that the fans stand up for the entire length of the game. You learn that this inflames the arthritis in your lower back and makes your sciatic nerve kill and you learn that you can never go to a game again, not that you would really want to anyway.

You learn that in the summer the girls wear very tiny bikini bottoms which you learn are much more flattering than big-butted bikini bottoms and you definitely copy that and are scandalous back on the beach in Maine before Brazilian cut bikinis break out on the scene in your own country.

You learn that wedding parties start around 10 PM and that there is dancing and music the whole entire time. You learn that weddings do not have a scheduled agenda and you learn to love this and think it is far superior to American style weddings where everything is so methodical and formulaic.

You learn that girls wear full length dresses to weddings, as fancy as something one would wear to the Oscars, and that they have their hair and makeup done and look like movie stars. However, you never learn why around 3 AM there is a part of the party called "cotillon" in which they break out funny hats and oversized sunglasses and start spraying each other with soapy bubble spray, ruining all the beautiful girls' hair and making them look like wilted walk of shamers when the party still has hours to go! You learn to hate this part and to hide when you see it starting so that your own hair and makeup won't get ruined. You learn that food is served throughout the whole night, first appetizers, then the main meal, then pizza and snack foods around 5 AM. The weddings don't end until way past sunrise. Your own isn't over until 7:30 in the morning but that was before you learned to not focus on your watch and getting up early so you felt like it dragged on for hours and you couldn't wait for it to be over. You were bored at your own wedding. You did learn to have a blast at subsequent weddings though, so you were very happy about that.

You learn that in this town, people don't have standing up parties. The parties you go to have very, very long tables that everyone sits around and you learn that when you arrive at these parties you must go around the table and greet each individual person with a kiss on the cheek. You must do the same when you leave as well. You think that although this is quite time-consuming, it is very nice and polite and you want to incorporate it into your own social life back home someday.

You learn that Prüne makes the best purses, Akiabara sells the best sweaters, Paula Cahen d'Anvers makes the best button-down shirts, Vandalia sells the best bikinis and Caro Cuore is WAY better than Victoria's Secret.

You learn that you strongly dislike dulce de leche, especially with chocolate, and you wish they would ever make desserts without it!

Those are some of the things you learn.

But most importantly, you learn to love so, so many people you meet there and you learn that that is the best lesson of all.

22 Watch Out for Argentine Hot Chocolate

When I first went to Argentina it was to take part in a cultural exchange program. I was going to teach at an English language institute and would be hosted by an Argentine family. I was placed in a family with two daughters, twelve year old Laura and nine year old Lucia. Their parents, Yely and Adolfo, picked me up at the airport in Buenos Aires and took me back to Santa Fe, four and half hours to the northwest. I was mesmerized looking out the window at the bright blue sky and the beautiful Argentine pampas, the green plains surrounding us as far as the eye could see, while Yely talked my ear off the entire trip home. I had studied Spanish ever since middle school and was already fluent, but the Argentine accent was so different from the Castillian Spanish I was used to. They also use a different conjugation for the second person than other Spanish speaking countries so I could barely understand a word she said to me! It was challenging at first but not for long; I picked it up quickly.

When we finally arrived at the house, I was introduced to their two daughters and it was pretty much love at first sight. We were like sisters from day one. Laura was a mature, responsible, achingly beautiful girl with brown hair, light brown eyes, a perfect nose and the weight of the world on her shoulders. Lucia was an adorable freckle-faced and kind-hearted little imp who did what she wanted without a care in the world and smothered me in the best way with kisses and cuddles. Despite their differences, those two were as close as two sisters could be and they generously extended their sisterly affection to me. I shared Laura's room with her and that was just fine with me. Who needs privacy when you are an only child who is finally getting the opportunity to share a bedroom with a little sister?

The first thing we did after I got settled was go to the grocery store, where Lucia pointed out to me all the things that were "rico." This was the first new word I learned there and it amused me that it was taught to me by a nine year old, but only because I misunderstood her. I had already known that "rico" meant "rich" in terms of wealth so as Lucia pointed out all her favorite foods to me, I assumed it also translated to "rich" in terms of succulent deliciousness. I thought Lucia certainly had a mature palate for a child to be pointing out all the "rich" foods. After a while it dawned on me that maybe I wasn't understanding her correctly. Yes, I understood that dulce de leche was "rich," but an apple? I asked Lucia to clarify. That was when I learned that it just meant "good," as in "delicioso," the word I was used to but not a word they really use in Argentina. Okay, so, rico=delicioso and Lucia was a normal child, not a connoisseur of haute cuisine. She was, however, very good and patient at explaining things to a confused American learning Argentine Spanish. The next word I learned was "cajero automátco" because I had no cash and needed to get money out of the ATM.

Yely and Adolfo hadn't bothered to mention previous to my arrival that they were going to be leaving the country a few days later for a three week trip to Canada and New York. I was a bit shocked at this news but Laura, Lucia and I didn't mind, it was already as if we had always known each other. Three girls with no parental supervision - that suited us just fine.

When Yely and Adolfo came back from Canada I got to experience family life again, this time with a Santafesina family. I loved dinners around the table in the evenings before I would rush off with Alejandro. Yely, a beautiful, elegant, and strongly opinionated woman, would initiate conversations about travelling, culture, and worldly matters. Yely was an observer, inquisitive, a citizen of the world who encouraged her daughters to be independent thinkers, as long as their thinking somewhat aligned with hers. Adolfo, the quieter one, would pipe in when prompted. On Friday nights we'd go out for ice cream at La Necochea where they'd treat me to my mint chocolate chip ice cream cone. We'd relax by their pool on the weekends, their yard a little private oasis enclosed in tall, ivy-covered brick walls. On Sunday nights, my favorite, we'd walk to the video store and rent a movie which we'd all watch together while eating the most delicious pizza, delivered from La Rotunda.

They took me on vacation to Mar del Plata where we jumped in the waves of the chilly Pacific. Afterwards, to warm up, they introduced me to Argentine hot chocolate, consisting of a glass of hot milk served with a bar of chocolate which you stir in until it melts. Unfortunately, it gave me the worst gas and poor Laura and Lucia had to breathe through their mouths all night as we laughed and I apologized.

They were also the ones who introduced me to Buenos Aires, that beautiful South American capital filled with tree-lined streets and neoclassical, beaux-arts, colonial and modern architecture. On a family trip there, Yely and Adolfo left us once again to our own devices while they had meetings to attend. They were raising their daughters to be independent, and I loved that about them. We took ourselves around, sightseeing, two little girls and an American, making our way just fine on our own.

Adolfo and Yely included me as if I were their daughter, Laura and Lucia as if I were their sister. I don't know how I was so lucky to end up with a family that fit me so well. Yely still calls me her American daughter. I've been back to visit many times. They have visited me in the States, both in Maine and DC. We even went on vacation to Brazil one year, driving the whole sixteen hours from Santa Fe in one shot, over the mountains, arriving at dawn. I thought I would sleep during that long drive but I couldn't take my eyes off that landscape even for a minute, first the flat and green pampas, then the hilly, lush mountains, then suddenly the blue of the coast. They took me to a different beach every day in Florianopolis, the Brazilian city where I learned that I can speak to someone in Spanish and they can respond to me in Portuguese and we can understand each other and have a conversation. I *also* learned in Brazil not to pluck my eyebrows so wide apart. That is a lesson I am very grateful for to the Brazilian women I observed.

This Santafesina family and I have memories together from Santa Fe, Mar del Plata, Buenos Aires, Brazil, Maine and Washington, DC. I may have not gotten to keep my Argentine husband but *this* family and these sisters are for life.

23 *I lost my virginity in Spain.*

The end of my marriage was not a happy time - the heartbreak, the failure, the missing, the empty bed. I don't know how I got through it. It certainly would have been a lot harder to without Quique (pronounced Kee-kay), to whom I will be forever grateful. Quique saved me. He also taught me to be the friend that I am today, a friend who checks in, reaches out, makes an effort, prioritizes relationships. He was a blessing in my life who reappeared just when I needed him the most.

Quique and Carlos were exchange students my senior year of high school. Quique was from Spain and Carlos was from Argentina. They were best friends. I crashed their twosome and we became an inseparable threesome. I had never had a real group of best friends before, always individual friends. Now I was part of a group and suddenly I had plans every weekend. Emily joined us and we became a foursome. Quique and Carlos became Quique and Jennifer and Carlos and Emily.

Quique taught us how to make Spanish tortilla, from Carlos we learned to make empanadas. I learned to capture life in photographs from them; it seemed like we were always taking trips to the mall to drop off film to be developed or to pick up photos. Carlos and Quique were the DJ's, constantly making mix tapes. U2's *Achtung Baby*, Pink Floyd's "Wish You Were Here" and Mercedes Sosa's "Gracias a la Vida" (Thanks to Life) became the soundtracks of our lives.

"Gracias a la Vida" is a beautiful Argentine folk song in which Mercedes Sosa recounts all the things life has given her - her eyes to see, her ears to hear, the path she has walked, her heart, laughter and tears. I didn't understand most of the lyrics at the time but the repetition of the words "gracias a la vida" fused themselves into my brain and made me more aware of the things for which I needed to be thankful. Would I be the same grateful person I am today if not for this Argentine folk singer from San Miguel de Tucumán who sang this life lesson to me, an American high school student in Portland, Maine, 5,000 miles away? Gracias a Mercedes Sosa for this song and this influence and to Carlos for introducing her to me.

Quique became fond of me as more than a friend. In fact, he fell in love with me. I was not in love, but I definitely liked him. God, I *really* liked him. We became intimate. My days became more exciting, my nights even more so. There were many firsts.

I was not ready to have that ultimate first though. He did not pressure me. But, he satisfied me. I never returned the favor; I didn't know what to do. This was before internet porn and I was innocent. I never even tried. He didn't seem to care.

I was a very responsible and trustworthy teenager. I never drank or partied. I actually have never been drunk in my life. My parents always knew where I was and I never gave them reason to worry. In return, they were so cool - when I finally had a life that required a curfew, they gave me a 2 AM curfew! Who gets that in high school?! For senior skip day I asked my parents if the four of us plus our other friends Josh and Sally could have a sleepover at our beach house. My parents said yes. A boy/girl sleepover with no adult supervision? How lucky were we? We spent the day on the beach, ordered Domino's delivery, and talked and laughed late into the night. I don't think there was even any alcohol involved. We were good kids. Even though Emily and I were having our first sleepovers with our boyfriends, I think we both ended that night with our virginities still intact. I am happy I grew up before society lost its innocence, when just the act of brushing our teeth together was, like, the most fun part of the whole night. I don't know why we laughed so hard or enjoyed that moment so much. Sometimes I guess it is just the simple things - the intimate yet simple act of brushing your teeth for the first time with your best friends.

When the school year ended and Carlos and Quique had to go back to their countries, Emily and I were devastated. The void they left was palpable. We were miserable. We missed our best friends, our innocent virginal lovers. I was luckier than Emily though because I had already planned on visiting Quique in Spain that summer. I was going there for five weeks. Poor Emily. I don't know how she handled those five weeks on her own.

Something clicked when I got to Spain and I saw him. My like turned into absolute, aching to the core of my being, love.

That handsome Spaniard with green eyes so light that they were practically yellow, invaded my heart and stayed there for half a decade until I finally, finally got over him. He was my first. Eighteen, in Spain, in his bed. I knew I had about one second to say "no" one more time, as I always had done before. But I couldn't say no. I loved him. I was ready.

Although my life didn't turn out as I had expected, there are certain moments I have gotten to live that have made me feel like the luckiest girl in the world, like when I met Alessandro in Italy and all my time as an au pair in France. I thought shooting stars were rare, but apparently, when you are lying on your back in a cornfield in Spain with the boy you love on top of you and you look up at the clear, dark sky full of stars, you learn that they are not, and your overwhelmed senses cause you to gasp. Balmy summer night, shooting stars in the sky, how good he feels inside you, this new sensation of which you want more and more. This is the type of moment that makes you thank God for being alive.

We were at his grandmother's house for a week in the countryside of Daimiel, a village in the province of Ciudad Real. The one hundred year old house, nicknamed El Recreo, was surrounded by cornfields, no other homes in sight. One day Quique took me hunting. Our prey were doves. Quique would shoot them and I would collect their little bodies; they barely weighed a thing. I was happy to be alone with him in the field but, man, what a boring activity. And, I felt like a dog running to retrieve the game. It was not glamorous! It was all worth it though when we brought them home and his grandmother and Carmen, the housekeeper who had served his family for four generations, prepared the meal. The doves, served over rice, were boiled in a broth of fried peppers, almonds, garlic, kidneys, livers and paprika. It was one of the most delicious meals I ever had in my life, served outside, next to the pool, surrounded by cornfields, in the middle of nowhere, Spain.

Another day, Quique took me on the back of his motorcycle to visit his other grandmother's house not far away in another village called Villarrubia de los Ojos. This home was a manor house, in the style called Casa Solariega, and was built in the 1600's. The walls and doors were so big and thick, it was like a fortress. When you stepped through the giant, paneled doors, you entered an interior courtyard, around which the house was built. The courtyard had a fountain in the middle and a mosaic floor. Quique came from a family of hunters and this house was full of game trophies from Spain and Angola. I remember the zebra rug on the floor in the living room and how much I loved the classic antique furniture, all from the 17th to 19th centuries. His family had purchased the home from a family of nobles 150 years prior. Walking around that beautiful home, I felt like I was in a museum. As I shamelessly took photographs of every detail, I realized that I definitely needed a 400 year old manor house of my own one day!

During our stay at El Recreo, every night Quique and his brother and I would sit outside by the pool, under the stars, and play a card game called Telefunken. This is a game you can play for money, one cent per point. I probably lost every time but I loved the game and by now I have taught it to almost everyone I know. I liked those quiet evenings, at that secluded spot in the Spanish countryside. I liked them a lot better than when we were in Madrid and we'd go out at night and I'd order a gin and tonic, like Quique. I never cared for alcohol and I hate carbonated beverages, but I didn't know what else to order so I just copied him. Yet, there I was, eighteen, in Spain, and I did feel grown-up, drinking my gin and tonic in a bar, out late at night.

An eighteen year old American girl, being shown the sites of Spain by a lovely Spanish family. How lucky was I? Madrid, Segovia, Toledo, Ciudad Real. Back in Madrid, they took me to the Prado where I saw paintings I had learned about in Spanish class with Señora Girr - Velasquez's *Las Meninas*, Goya's *The Third of May 1808*, Picasso's *La Guernica*. It was so exciting to see those paintings I had learned about in a classroom in Portland, Maine, over 3,000 miles away.

I loved Quique's parents and his brother Alvaro. I loved their apartment, decorated with antler trophies, lots of plants and two couches facing each other. I have wanted two couches facing each other ever since. I am going to have that someday.

It was 1992 and the summer Olympics were being held in Spain that year. That was the first time that NBA players were allowed to compete and *everyone* was excited about the Dream Team. I remember that we couldn't wait for the games to begin that year so that we could be riveted by the greatest sports team in history competing on the world stage. We knew that team of household name superstars, who normally competed against each other, would work together to effortlessly crush the competition and that is exactly what they did. It was exhilarating. I am not even a sports fan and I was glued to the TV, switching back and forth between those two couches as Michael Jordan, Magic Johnson, Scottie Pippen, Charles Barkley, David Robinson and Larry Bird ran up and down the court.

Though there were good moments on this trip, it was actually one of the most painful times in my life. I was in Spain with Quique, but our roles had switched. Now I was the one in love and he was detaching himself. Back in his own country, adjusting back to his own culture, reuniting with missed friends, thoughts of college and his future on his mind. I was there with him but he was not actually present. I was young and I didn't know how to process all the emotions I was feeling - love, change, loss, desire, neediness. It was very hard. His change toward me and his lack of attention broke my heart, daily.

I cried uncontrollably the entire way back to the States. I wrote him letters every single day. I wrote and I wrote but when I checked my mailbox it was empty. Empty and empty and empty. Almost always empty. I think he wrote me four letters. Ever. He broke my heart again and again. I finally gave up.

It was right after Alejandro left me, when I was struggling with the pain of separation, that was the precise moment that Quique reappeared in my life, having found me on Facebook. He contacted me. Quique. The boy I had pined for and cried over who hurt me like no one had ever hurt me. There he was. I got to tell him how he had made me feel. How I had ached for him. How disappointed I was that he hadn't even tried to stay friends. He apologized. I forgave. And then he gave me back everything he had taken: he gave me the friendship I needed when I needed it the most.

Quique emailed me every single day while I was going through that awful period. Every morning when I woke up and checked my Blackberry there was a message from him telling me I would get through it, things would be okay, to stay strong, "Fuerza!" Knowing that he cared and that he thought of me saved me in that sad and lonely time. He called me his Lovely Downer. There is no way to describe the gratitude I feel toward him for his support at that time. When I started building a social life and going out all the time, thanks to my roommates (coincidentally at that time, The Dream Team, although a different one, re-appeared in my life), I entertained him with my stories of my dating adventures in between lamenting how much I missed Alejandro. He told me I was "Lovely Downer by day and Catwoman by night." Quique was always good at nicknames and he made me laugh through my tears. Seventeen years later, he reappeared into my life just when I needed him the most. You just never, ever know what can happen.

24 Not. On. Purpose.

It's kind of ironic that the person I lost my virginity to was two years older than me. Aside from Quique and my college boyfriend Scott, who was only eleven months older than me, I have never been with anyone else older. First, there was Michael; apparently he was prologue to my various trysts with guys younger than me. I swear it isn't on purpose! It has just worked out that way. When I match with younger guys on dating apps, I often get asked "So, you are into younger guys?" I hate that question. How do you even answer that? Should I give them my whole life story so that they can know how true that apparently is? I just tell them "I like attractive, fit guys." I mean, duh. It's not my fault they usually turn out to be younger.

I met Jeremy my senior year in college when I was out one night and Scott and I were on a break. Jeremy was *hot* – with hair that was dirty blonde and eyes that were blue, he was tall and muscular. We met at a dance club. He knew how to flirt, a rare and much appreciated skill. He came back to my dorm with me and we fooled around all night, no sleeping. He was in DC for the weekend from school in Pennsylvania where he was a sophomore. I really liked him; the feeling was mutual. We met up again the next day and hung out before he went back to school.

Given that Jeremy was from Texas and went to school in Pennsylvania, we didn't have plans to see each other again but we were fond of each other and kept in touch. We wrote each other letters and talked on the phone once in a while, a big deal in those days when long-distance phone calls were expensive! The following summer after coming home from my time as an au pair in France, I called Jeremy to see how he was doing. The housekeeper answered and told me he wasn't home. I asked if she could tell me when he would be back. She said that he wouldn't be back for a week - he was in Spain with his sister celebrating his eighteenth birthday.

Um, his EIGHTEENTH??

Wait.

Calculate.

So, he was in high school when we met? No wonder the bouncer had said his ID was fake when we tried to get into that bar! So yeah, Jeremy. Sixteen year old Jeremy who went to school in Pennsylvania - boarding school that is! A high school sophomore! I had been 22, he was sixteen. This seems to be the story of my life.

When my ex-husband and I separated the first time I was thirty and ended up dating a 21 year old. After we separated for the final time, I was 34 and still dating guys in their twenties. At 41 my boyfriend of six years was 34. At 43 I was still dating and being intimate with 25 year olds. Ten years older than the last time I'd been with a 25 year old but still, those were my "conquests." I mean, heck, at 42 I had spent the night with a nineteen year old! Although, I have to admit, if your reality is to be in your forties and single and life did not work out in any way as you had wanted or expected, it definitely helps to know that at least you can have a Roster of Not Boyfriends who are under thirty, and sometimes you can even unwittingly throw a British nineteen year old into the mix.

25 Sometimes Age Really Is Just a Number

I thought with Jason I was going to be safe. He was the one person I dated who was almost age appropriate. He was 37, I was 42. We had nine dates. He was a total gentleman on every one. For our first date we went for a walk around the National Mall. He talked my ear off about his job and family and world travels and I enjoyed listening to his stories. At the end, I especially liked that he did not try to manhandle me; I didn't have to dodge any preemptive kisses.

Our second date was a spontaneous dinner date the next week. He treated me to a restaurant I had been wanting to try. In fact, he paid every time we went out. I never had to spend a penny. I appreciated that very much; it was so nice to be treated that way and was not something I was used to. He was very generous with me. He had done most of the talking on our first date but this time he did most of the listening. He seemed interested in what I had to say and wanted to know about me which was nice. I felt charming and comfortable talking to him. I wasn't sure if I felt a spark but I was enjoying myself in his company and he seemed like he was enjoying my company too. After dinner, he walked me to the metro and he hugged me goodbye. Then, he took a step back, looked me intensely in the eye, and then just grabbed my face with both hands and went in for a kiss. It was like a movie scene, very romantic and very hot. I *definitely* felt a spark then, more like fireworks!

Jason was handsome, smart, extremely well-travelled, a former Division One football player and a former Navy SEAL. He was 220 pounds of pure muscle. I liked a lot about him. He was Not Nathan, but I felt that given our ages, there was potential for something real and I wanted to take our time, get to know each other and see. I felt safe with him because I assumed that, given his age and the fact that he had a little daughter and sisters, he would be respectful of me as a woman, as a human. Well, I was wrong.

The last time I saw Jason, it was at a dinner party at my apartment. I made dinner and had him and some friends over. I was excited to introduce Jason to my friends and excited that he was even willing to meet them, as people put up such boundaries nowadays. Jason was charming and so funny at dinner. He made us all laugh with his stories until our stomachs hurt. I felt good sitting next to him. I was proud of the friends I had over and the meal that I served and it was nice to share that with a man I also felt proud to sit next to. Despite having fun with my friends, I looked forward to them leaving so that I could be alone with Jason and he could have his way with me.

I really liked my intimacy with Jason. He was not quiet; he was very communicative and complimentary. I can't stand when guys are silent. It is not relaxing at all because you have no idea if they are enjoying themselves or bored. And, I need positive reinforcement. I don't need them to build my confidence, I just need confirmation that they realize they are lucky to be with me and that they are enjoying me. Jason was excellent at that. He was also very strong and I just loved the feeling of being pinned down by him, of him being able to do as he pleased, and the fact that he could hurt me if he wanted to but wouldn't, well, at least not physically.

The next morning when he left, he gave me some very nice kisses which I thought were "I like you" kisses - that was what they felt like. But, I misunderstood those kisses. Apparently, they were goodbye kisses because I never saw him again.

He started to ignore me. At first, it was confusing. I didn't know if I was being ignored or if he was busy. I hate being confused. And being ignored is the worst. I just hate it. I think it is such a cruel tactic to use on another human being. He was definitely Not Nathan.

I asked him to please just stop ignoring me, to just tell me if he was busy or if he just didn't like me anymore.

He finally responded. On Christmas Eve he texted me and told me:

> While I really like being around (in ☺) you, I don't think pursuing a romantic relationship with each other is in our cards right now.

Blindside. We had never had one unpleasant moment between us so I did not see that coming and I certainly didn't expect to be dumped by text from someone who had been out with me nine times, who had been intimate with me, who was 37 years old for goodness sake! It really, really hurt me to be treated that way. I told him I appreciated him being honest but that I wished he could have told me in person or at least on the phone (I mean, seriously??!! Paul who was ten years *younger* than Jason and who I had only been on *two* dates with had had the decency to *call* me to tell me he decided he didn't want a third! I appreciated that – it actually made me *happy* because he treated me with respect which enabled me to respect *him*. So much better!!). Jason told me he would have preferred to tell me on the phone or in person as well but that he didn't have that "option right now," whatever that meant.

I had no idea what happened. He didn't give me any reasons. I wrote back various messages, none of them mean or angry, really just asking for closure. He gave me none. He just didn't respond.

He put me in the position of wondering, of questioning myself. I went over every exchange we had had trying to figure out what I might have done or said that would have caused him to do this. I couldn't figure it out. Had I pressured him? No. Did he hate my cooking? I didn't think so. I believe he had thirds! My friends? No, I didn't think that was it. Did he meet someone else? I didn't think so because he was incredibly busy between his job and his children.

It wasn't nice. He discarded me and ignored me, not only like I didn't matter to him, but like I didn't matter at *all*. It was very cruel.

Because I wasn't enamored by him or attached to him, since on my own end I had still been deciding how I felt about him, I wasn't heartbroken over not having him in my life anymore. However, *he* didn't know that and he still hurt me very badly by the *way* he ended things. It is hard to be single and put yourself out there. And since I had cast a wide net as a favor to my future self, I had exposed myself to the potential for a lot of unkindness and I really didn't need one more bad experience to pile on top of all the others. In one of my unanswered messages, I told him:

> When someone tells you they like you, and is vulnerable to you, you should be more gentle with them. Being handled in this manner makes me feel hopeless and makes me afraid to put myself out there and makes me want to put up walls and I don't want to be that way. So be aware, that how you treat someone doesn't just affect them in relation to you, but can in relation to the world.

Can people just realize that? Can we all just be good representatives of our genders? Can we just treat each other with human kindness? Like, seriously? Why is that so hard?

It bothered me that I didn't have closure. That he never gave me a reason.

Until finally, he did. Three months later.

For three months he ignored me. Then one night, out of the blue, he told me why. Blindsided again, his reasons made me glad I hadn't been heartbroken over him. He had three or four and they were all a result of either him projecting onto me, misunderstanding me, or being dishonest about his own feelings and setting me up for failure. So that was that. I had closure. And from his closure, I learned that not only was he emotionally immature, but that he was also a horrible communicator, on top of already knowing that he was incredibly inconsiderate and unkind, all of which meant he was definitely not the guy for me. If he had just talked to me about any of the things he decided to blow me off for, they could have just been easily explained and resolved and we could have kept dating or he could have saved me three months of unpleasant wondering. But no. Like my friend and former roommate Sarah told me once, "Rejection is protection." Yep, it sure is.

What did I do? I thanked him for finally being honest with me and told him I appreciated it very much.

And then I went back to swiping on 25 year olds.

26 Moscow Part 1

Hooks. I hung up a new hook in my apartment recently. I am more excited about that hook than I am about the last few dates I went on. I can't stop thinking about that hook. When I started having roommates, I needed to hang up more hooks for people's towels. It is empowering to be able to hang up hooks by yourself when you don't have a man in your life to help you. You know where they have a lot of hooks? Moscow. There is never not a place to hang something on a hook if you need a hook in Moscow. I have never been anywhere with so many convenient hooks.

I have gotten to go to Moscow twice. It was so exciting that first time, seeing Red Square and being behind the "Iron Curtain." Growing up in the '80's, we were terrified of Russia starting a nuclear war with us. This fear was always in the back of my mind and it was scary and stressful. I found solace in Sting's song "Russians." The song talks about the fact that since the Russians must love their children too, they couldn't want to actually blow up the world. Whenever that song came on the radio, it made me feel so much better. I taped it off the radio so I could listen to it over and over and calm myself. I hoped Sting was right.

It is funny how a song can save you. Madonna saved me with her *Erotica* album. I was suffering from a terrible broken heart my freshman year of college. I listened to that album over and over, almost every song on it seemed to have been written just to help me get through that time.

> But your actions speak louder than words
> And they're only words, unless they're true
> Your actions speak louder than promises
> You're inclined to make and inclined to break

Those songs comforted me and gave me strength. Thank you, Madonna.

Solace can be found in many places. A song, a friend reaching out unexpectedly, or during that awful time my freshman year, every night having my mom read me my favorite book, Roald Dahl's *The Giraffe, the Pelly, and Me,* over the phone so that I could fall asleep. That helped a lot.

When you have a broken heart for the first time it is all-consuming, physically painful and you feel like you will NEVER feel better, like it will never go away and you will never feel happy again. Your first broken heart is scary but you learn that with time, you do feel better eventually. Broken hearts are never easy, but that first one? When you are young and inexperienced? That is the worst.

Music that touches you, friends who reach out, activities that distract you: these are good coping mechanisms for broken hearts. I also like to have imaginary conversations.

27 Imaginary Conversations

I've actually spent a lot of time having imaginary conversations. Sometimes these conversations are just for entertainment, but sometimes they are to help me cope. I'm not a drinker so I need to find escape in different ways. Endless hours of TV help the time pass when you are trying to heal wounds. Binge-watching ten hours of Netflix gets me ten hours of distance from whatever upset me, which helps. However, going for a walk and having an imaginary conversation is much better exercise and burns more calories than sitting on the couch.

I spent hours and hours and hours entertaining myself with conversations with Imaginary Michael when I was growing up. Imaginary Michael and I took so many walks on the beach, he would come surprise me in the outside shower after the beach, he visited me in France when I lived there and went all over with me. I had a whole future planned out with Imaginary Michael. When I found out that he had gotten his girlfriend pregnant back in 2002, my journal entry for that day was "Found out that Michael is going to be a father. My reaction was HOW COULD HE DO THIS TO ME??? There goes my fantasy world - in the uterus of a nineteen year old."

When I lived in Venice, there was Imaginary Alejandro, keeping me company on Caterina's cell phone as I walked around that aquatic labyrinth. At that time, our conversations were pleasant and fun and romantic. Later, I am sure that Imaginary Alejandro and I spent a lot of time discussing all the things we were fighting about, trying so hard to understand each other.

I used this technique when I was trying to deal with the frustration of not seeing Nathan anymore. Imaginary Nathan would call me on the phone when I was out taking walks or driving home from work. He told me all the things that I ached to hear. He changed his mind. He wanted to see me. He wanted me to come over for John Oliver and pizza. He wanted to go to Miami for a weekend with me. He told me how much he appreciated all the aspects of my personality of which I am most proud.

The good thing about imaginary conversations is that when the person is no longer in your life, you run out of imaginary things to talk about. And when you have run out of things to say, the frustration at not being with them lessens. And eventually, you don't need your imaginary versions of them anymore.

I'm not going to lie though, Imaginary Nathan and I still hang out sometimes. Yesterday he announced that he is taking me first class to Paris tomorrow. I was down with that.

28 Moscow Part 2

But yes, back to Moscow. The first time I went was to visit
Alexei, roommate number ten at my International Youth Hostel,
who had become one of my best friends almost immediately
upon moving in. Our personalities just clicked. Alexei had this
t-shirt of a cartoon raccoon on it and the raccoon happened to
look just like him. I endearingly called him my Little Raccoon.
(Coincidentally, when I was little and my parents and I would

drive to Lewiston to visit my grandparents, we had a CB radio in the car to entertain us. I don't how know they came up with it, but my handle was Little Raccoon Girl. I remembered this long after I had given Alexei his nickname - I guess we were just destined to be dear friends). Alexei lived with me during the summer so we spent a lot of time just hanging out together up at my rooftop pool, looking at fashion magazines and talking about our very confusing significant others, trying to make sense of them.

Alexei had grown up half in America, half in Russia but he preferred Russia and moved back there after living with me. The first time I visited him was to help take his mind off his broken heart after his girlfriend, with whom he was madly in love, broke up with him. Since I am an expert at knowing what it is like to suffer from a broken heart, I applied for my Russian visa, got my plane ticket and was on my way. I visited for ten days and Alexei took the whole time off work to be my tour guide. I distracted him and he showed me Moscow. Despite the circumstances being less than ideal for him, I was thrilled to be there, "behind the iron curtain," this place that seemed so forbidden when I was growing up. It was strange to be in a country where I couldn't even read the street signs or communicate with anyone. I was totally dependent on Alexei, who took me all over that city. It was a new experience, as I had never before travelled somewhere I couldn't speak the language - I have been a polyglot since college, able to communicate in four languages.

My favorite thing about Moscow was the metro. The Moscow metro runs efficiently and is very inexpensive. They have free WiFi in their metro! I can barely get a signal for data I *pay* for in the DC metro! The trains run constantly; if you have to wait four minutes you feel burdened, unlike in DC where sometimes you are expected to wait thirty minutes for a train on a Friday night! I also didn't see any metros catch on fire, have to single-track, or offload. Their metro just *works*.

The escalators are extremely deep and steep and they move faster than the ones I am used to in DC. At the bottom of the escalator there is a little booth where a person wearing a uniform sits and yells at you on a loudspeaker if you stand on the left and block the way. Russians love their uniforms. They have way more uniformed people than we do, from the public employees to the police and army to the wait-staff in restaurants. They are properly and elegantly uniformed and usually have a matching hat. I loved that, especially the hats.

Aside from the practical functionality of the Moscow metro, it is beautiful. One of the stations is so beautiful that tears literally formed in my eyes and escaped down my face the first time I saw it. Before I went to Moscow, I used to say that the DC metro was the most beautiful metro in the world. I don't know what facts I based that opinion on since I think the only other metro system I had ever seen was the New York subway. I just knew that DC's was more attractive and modern looking than New York's and that since it was better than New York's and in *America*, that meant it had to be the most beautiful in the world. Right?

Wrong.

While I do like the elegant Brutalist uniformity of the DC metro, it is absolutely *not* the most beautiful. It doesn't even compare to Moscow's. Or St. Petersburg's, for that matter. Moscow's metro is not even one of the most beautiful metros in the world, it is one of the most beautiful *things* in the world. It is also proof that not *everything* west of the Iron Curtain is better.

I always tell people, you could go to Russia and ONLY ride the metro and you would have an amazing vacation. Each station is unique and features a different kind of art: sculpture, mosaics, stained glass, friezes, statues made of marble or bronze, and bas-reliefs. You can be dazzled by the fact that every station has a different lighting concept from chandeliers, to lamps on poles, to lights in ceiling coffers. The design of the lighting alone can take your breath away. Even the ventilation grates in the Moscow metro are beautifully adorned. You can learn so much about Russian history and culture and art from the metro. You can see all the Soviet pride, their hammer and sickle and five pointed star are *everywhere*. As I rode the metro, I was impressed by their nationalism and I wondered why despite being so "USA! USA! USA!" all the time we don't have more American flags and eagles adorning our public spaces. I was jealous. We should *do* that!

There are a lot of depictions of weapons in the metro, weapons used in the World Wars. I think their depiction is to reassure the Russians that they are safe, that the state will protect them, especially after suffering so much trauma from the Nazi invasion in World War II. Aside from weapons and historical figures, there are all sorts of depictions of Russian men, women and children playing sports or performing arts or science, of people being industrious, males and females working together. These portrayals of equal participation in society by the sexes was very surprising to see, since I am used to history, industry and sports in the United States being so male dominated. It made Russia seem so modern, so civilized.

I would have liked to have spent so much more time in the metro, learning who all the historic figures were, depicted in the paintings and mosaics and tile work and stained glass and bronzes and about the artists who created them. How amazing is it that Stalin believed so strongly in funding all of this artwork, to be enjoyed by all the people who rode the metro? Someday I would love to study about the artists and artisans who were employed to decorate these stations that are described as looking like palaces. There must have been a lot of them and they must have been incredibly busy because they did A LOT of work!

The metro is also a great place for people watching. I noticed there that Russians have amazing eye colors, different shades of light browns and greens and blues that I'd never seen in the States. I wanted to just stare at them all and try to figure out what the names of those colors would be. If someone caught me staring at their eyes, I would smile. They wouldn't smile back. Russians NEVER SMILE at strangers. I was told that is because they only smile when they are happy, only when it is genuine. They don't smile just to be friendly. They must have all thought I was crazy because the less they smiled, the more I smiled, trying to elicit a little upturn of the corners of a mouth. I failed. Every time. They are steadfast in their refusal to smile at a stranger.

One day, Alexei took me to meet his coworkers for lunch. They spoke a little English so it was fun to talk to them about the similarities and differences between our two cultures. One of Alexei's coworkers had traveled to the States and he told me how impressed and intrigued he was by how polite and smiley Americans are. Given that he wasn't used to seeing his own comrades smile, he wondered why Americans seemed to be smiling all the time. He told me it was something he pondered a lot while he was in the States, considering various reasons why it might be the case. Finally, the explanation that he came up with? It must be because of the Second Amendment. Clearly, everyone must be friendly and smiling because no one ever knows who's carrying a gun. My jaw dropped at that analysis. It says a lot about cultural perspective and a Russian's perception of Americans.

Ever since I was little during the Cold War, I dreamed of someday seeing Red Square. I don't know what caused me to be so fascinated by this place. Maybe because it was "behind enemy lines?" Maybe it was the architecture of St. Basel's? And then one day, seemingly all of a sudden, there I was, standing in Red Square. But, it wasn't sudden. It was a result of a series of events and decisions, some in my control, some just as a result of my own particular orbit.

I like to think about how I end up places I never expected to be. It is fun to consider all the things that had to align in order for me to be there. If Señora Girr hadn't been such a good Spanish teacher in high school in Maine, I wouldn't have majored in Spanish and Latin American Studies in college. If I hadn't chosen that major, I wouldn't have gone to Argentina to do a cultural exchange. If I hadn't been sent to Santa Fe, 5,000 miles away from home, I wouldn't have met my Argentine husband. If I hadn't married my husband, I wouldn't have bought my apartment. If my husband hadn't divorced me, I wouldn't have ended up with a Russian living in my living room. And, if I hadn't lived with Alexei, I wouldn't have travelled another almost 5,000 miles to Moscow. The list could go on and on about all the factors that ended me up in that spot at that time. I had travelled almost 15,000 miles to end up somewhere 5,000 miles away. Red Square was beautiful and I was very happy to be there and grateful to Señora Girr and Yely and Adolfo and Alejandro and Alexei and myself for getting me there.

Alexei and I also visited St. Petersburg. We took the train there, over a seven hour trip. If you look at a map of Russia, St. Petersburg and Moscow do not look that far apart. That is because they are not, in relation to the size of Russia as a whole. That was when I learned that Russia is HUGE. It has eleven time zones! It is the largest country in the world! It is almost twice as big as the United States! I had not known that!

Like Venice, St. Petersburg is a city that seems to have all been built at the same time, its uniformly baroque and neoclassical buildings look as if they had just magically popped up all at once. I loved the beautiful uniformity of the architecture. I enjoyed seeing Catherine's Palace, the Summer Palace, The Hermitage, Putin's dacha and the St. Petersburg metro.

Mostly, I loved meeting Alexei's friend Annya who lives in St. Petersburg and was our gracious and glamorous tour guide. She took us all around the city and did so wearing a dress with fishnets and heels. I marveled at her femininity and wanted to emulate her, though touring a city in heels is not something I think I will ever be able to accomplish. When we took pictures, Annya didn't just stand and smile like an American would. She posed as if she were a model in a fashion magazine. As we spent the day walking around, I noticed that other Russian tourists who were taking pictures were doing the same thing. I thought it was so funny but also, seriously, why NOT pose like a model in a fashion magazine when you are taking photos? Why DON'T we do that?

I loved meeting Annya and observing her ways, incorporating her into my list of people who have influenced me. After that amazing trip and my cherished time with Alexei, what was the first thing I did when I got back to the United States?

Bought a pair of fishnets.

29 Moscow Part 3 (Hedonism with Friends)

The second time I went to Moscow was for Alexei's wedding. I got to go to a *wedding* in *Russia!* Alexei found someone way better for him than the girl he was originally brokenhearted over during my first visit. Olga was beautiful, sweet, sexy, smart and also adorable and affectionate. She was Alexei's dream girl and I was so happy for him. I had met her the summer before, when they came to the U.S. for vacation and visited a few days in Washington. It was so great to be with Alexei in DC again and to see him so happy. After spending three days together, when Olga said goodbye to me she teared up. She did not want to say goodbye and I didn't want to either. Her expression of emotion, especially given that she is Russian and therefore only lets her face reflect genuine feelings, made me feel so special and meant so much to me, as I was very lonely for friends at that time. I love warm, expressive people and I was so glad that Alexei was marrying one. I wish we all lived closer!

On that second trip to Moscow I didn't have Alexei all to myself like the first time. That time we were joined by his other best friends: Ollé from Sweden, Yury from Belarus, and Jane from Minnesota. I actually had met all of them before briefly when Alexei lived with me and Yury had actually become roommate number 34, living with me a few years after Alexei had. I hadn't seen him since, so it was nice to be reunited again. Yury used to do pushups every morning and because of this, he got added to the list of people who have influenced me in some way, as I incorporated morning pushups into my own routine. Every day before I leave for work, the last three things I do are perfume, pushups, pee. The alliteration helps me remember. Thanks Yury!

I felt so special and honored to be included in this group, especially since Alexei had known these friends much longer than he had known me. We spent our days sightseeing and our evenings trying new and chic restaurants, calling our activities Hedonism with Friends. The exchange rate from the dollar to the ruble was very good and even better for Ollé's Swedish krona so we were able to enjoy without being worried about money. Ollé took full advantage of this and ordered everything on the menu that his heart (and stomach) desired with the intention to *try* and not necessarily to finish. I hate the idea of wasting food but I am also incorporating this into my repertoire of influences. When on vacation, exposed to the opportunity to try new things, why choose? Gluttony from Ollé, pushups from Yury. It *should* balance out, right?

I usually associate the word "exotic" with palm trees and warm breezes, not Arctic Circle fish liver, but there is no other word to describe all the new foods I got to try in Russia. Venison served slightly frozen so that when you place it on your tongue, it literally melts in your mouth? Hot smoked eel and pressed catfish. Salad topped with rabbit livers. Fried eggplant stuffed with walnuts and pomegranate. Duck carpaccio with turnip and sea buckthorn. Duck and game dumplings. Salad with snake-root knotgrasses, arugula and pumpkin. Siberian game blintz. Deer tongue. Quail, northern deer, and Siberian stag patés. And the best of all, a meal I ate twice in one day for both lunch and dinner: duck with cherry sauce and cherry risotto accompanied by foie gras raviolis and apricot stuffed pear.

Aside from enjoying our Hedonism with Friends, I had an additional mission. I needed to buy drugs. Ever since I was fifteen years old, I have suffered from arthritis in my lower back which used to cause me terrible, crippling sciatic pain. It took years and years before I was diagnosed. I thank GOD for my opthamologist because he was the one who actually figured out what was causing my sciatica.

By the time I was in my early thirties, I had gotten to the point where I was literally disabled. I couldn't do ANYTHING other than sit at my desk at work and sit at my dining table at home. I was in terrible pain all the time and there were so many triggers: standing, walking slowly, sitting on anything soft (I didn't sit on my couch for YEARS), etc. etc. My quality of life was terrible and it was very, very depressing to be young and not be able to do hardly anything. In addition to the terrible pain in my legs, my eyes would also hurt me every so often. Because of the pain in my eyes, I went to see Dr. Pluznik. He diagnosed me as having iritis, an inflammation of the eye, easily taken care of with drops.

However, he said that iritis is an arthritic condition and that maybe my sciatic pain I had told him about was a result of that too. He suggested I make an appointment with a rheumatologist and he changed my life.

I immediately made an appointment with Dr. Wolfe and he indeed confirmed that I was suffering from some kind of arthritic condition. He prescribed me a non-steroidal anti-inflammatory drug called Indomethacin and suddenly I could enjoy life again without being in constant, crippling pain. I could finally sit on the couch again and watch TV! Not only did the medicine relieve my suffering, it practically cured me. I don't have to take it regularly, only as needed which, as long as I am very active, is not often. I also can't remember the last time I got iritis. I just want to give Dr. Pluznick a giant hug whenever I see him. Out of all the internists and orthopedists and specialists I saw, he was the one who figured it out. How do you measure gratitude for someone whose thorough attention gave you your life back?

When I first started taking Indomethacin, it cost me $5 for 120 pills. Over the years, with insurance benefits becoming worse and worse (or was it that medicine was becoming more expensive?), it eventually got to the point that sixty pills cost me $143. Not only that, but I needed a prescription and in order to get one, it meant I had to spend a $40 copay for a five minute office visit that seemed totally unnecessary to me. This was too much! Having lived abroad, I know that medicine is cheaper and more easily accessible in other countries so I figured I would take advantage of my trip to Moscow and turn Alexei into my dealer. He was amused by the way that sounded and, being the supportive friend he is, he ooked up procuring me the drugs. Well, apparently in Russia, Indomethacin can be ordered online, without a prescription and fifty pills cost $3.75!

My first day there, Alexei ordered me four boxes, at least a year's supply. A few hours later, we were out for lunch and he got a phone call. He spoke authoritatively to the person on the other end, sounding like he was giving directions. When he hung up, I asked him what that was about. "Your drugs. They'll be here in a few minutes. Get the cash ready." Yeah, so not only were we able to order my medicine online, without a prescription, but just two hours later they were also going to be *delivering* it to us, at a *restaurant* and the whole deal was going to cost me just $15 for a year's supply. Mission accomplished.

While we were at the restaurant, I wanted to purchase a pretty box of sweets that they had in a display case. I thought it would be a nice souvenir. However, the box had apparently been in the display case for so long that the sweets inside were expired, and therefore, the waiter said that they couldn't sell it to me. I had Alexei explain that I didn't care about the sweets, I just wanted the box so could they please just sell me that? They refused and told him that they were not allowed to sell us an empty box. There was a lot of pleading and negotiations until they finally conceded to allow me to have the box if I would buy enough of other non-expired sweets they were selling that would add up to the value of the box that I wanted.

Yes! Fine!

Ironically, there seemed to be more regulation around me buying an *empty* box than around me buying drugs. Additionally, the three boxes of sweets I needed to buy actually cost more than twice as much as my year supply of the drugs! But, I got my box and now I have a place to put my drugs, the juxtaposition of those two events decorating my nightstand, literally tied up with a bow.

Aside from the sightseeing and the eating and the drug buying, the purpose of this trip was to attend Alexei's wedding. I was so excited to be invited to a wedding in Russia and to have a new cultural experience. Alexei's wedding did not disappoint.

Compared with an Argentine wedding party, the festivities

started very early. It was still daylight as everyone stood outside waiting to throw rose petals on the ground for the bride and groom as they approached the party venue. Also, unlike Argentine weddings, this wedding was very structured. They had an MC who moved the party along through all the party parts. Unfortunately, since it was all in Russian, I couldn't really understand what was happening most of the time. There were a lot of games played and it reminded me more of a Bar or Bat Mitzvah than a wedding. There wasn't as much dancing as I had expected and I don't think I saw a single person drinking vodka.

Since few Russians speak English, I was very pleased to find I was seated at a table next to a very nice couple who were indeed fluent and I was able to talk with them about our cultural differences and ask their impressions of Americans. We seem to have so much in common with Russia: we are both into being superpowers and having big militaries, we are civilized, we excel at sports and we are very nationalistic. Because of this, it is strange to me that we are not best friends, so I wanted to inquire about how they saw us and how they saw themselves. First, I asked them how Russians perceive Americans. They said that their propaganda portrays us as being "stupid and not knowing geography." That made me laugh. I asked them to tell me the best things and the worst things about Russians. They said that Russians are very open and they have the "Russian soul." They explained that this means that they are very passionate and warm people. That surprised me, given their reluctance to smile at strangers, making them seem so cold to me. I was glad to hear that that was not the case and was instead an interesting misperception. The worst thing? "We kill people we hate." That made me laugh too. Oh boy.

The best part of the wedding was the bride and groom's first dance. Alexei and Olga's first dance, however, was *not* typical for a Russian wedding. Having sneakily disappeared for a bit, they reappeared, no longer dressed in their wedding attire, temporarily exchanging it for more comfortable clothes. They then proceeded to delight their guests with a surprise aerial silks performance. The bride and groom's first dance entailed them spinning in the air together, timed perfectly to Seal's "Kissed by a Rose" and resulted in me being covered with goose bumps. There was an audible, collective gasp as everyone's breath was taken away. The best part was that though Olga had been practicing aerial silks for years, Alexei had spent the last nine months secretly learning the routine with her so that, in addition to awing his guests with this surprise, he could make his bride's dream of an airborne first dance come true. It was so beautiful - beautiful to watch and a beautiful gesture. The guests were stunned and dazzled. I felt *so* lucky to be there.

The day after the wedding I took a car back to the airport. I had spent ten days in Moscow where I didn't have a moment of the loneliness that so often plagued my life in DC. I enjoyed Hedonism with Friends, took pleasure in trying new and delicious foods, luxuriated in beautiful restaurants with cutting edge interior design, soaked up the sites of Moscow, and delighted in the company of this international group of elegant people. On my way to the airport, watching the sunrise over the Russian landscape, heading back to my life in DC, to an apartment that I was still sharing with roommates eight years after my husband left and to navigating the misery of the dating app world, I once again found myself alone in the backseat.

30 The Second Kind of First Date

I have learned that there are four kinds of first dates. Some dates you go on and you have a pleasant enough time while you wait for the date to be over. Some dates you go on and you have the best time on planet earth with someone who you never need to see again. Some dates you go on and you need another date to decide how you feel. And, some dates you go on and want that person to be your boyfriend immediately: Nathan.

Apparently to David, his date with me was the second kind of first date. David was a 26 year old who lived in my neighborhood. I wanted to meet him: a. because he lived nearby and b. because he spoke Spanish fluently and I thought it would be great to have someone with whom to practice. He was cuter in real life than in his profile pictures, strawberry blonde hair accompanying a face that looked like it could have been on the cover of "Yachting" magazine or some such boat themed journal. We spent our entire date speaking in Spanish.

We met at a bar in the neighborhood and sat at a table outside in the sun, getting to know each other in a foreign language. Enjoying each other's company, the date progressed to taking a walk. I showed him where our neighborhood park is that has a chin-up bar and we had a competition. We swung across the monkey bars at the playground. I think there may even have been some handstands as well. I liked his vibe. I liked talking to him. I was having fun. But, I had something else on my mind: ice cream.

I think I have some sort of ice cream curse. Whichever ice cream is my favorite, the grocery store discontinues. First, it was Häagen Dazs Chocolate Covered Pomegranate Bars. Then, it was Talenti Chocolate Covered Raspberry Bars. Now, it was my ultimate, all-time favorite: Giant brand Chocolate Chocolate Chip Lowfat Greek Frozen Yogurt. That was the best ice cream I had ever had in America. So, when I went to the grocery store on my way home from work that day, I became distraught upon finding out that it was on sale for $1.75 a pint (!!!) because it was being DISCONTINUED. Whyyyyyy? Why me? Why meeeeeeeeeeee??????

After that panic-inducing discovery, I stopped at the second Giant I passed on my commute in order to buy all that they had left in stock. I got seven pints at the first Giant and then three more at the second. When I got home, I put the ten pints in my freezer which did nothing whatsoever to alleviate my anxiety or console me as I mourned the impending loss of that heavenly chocolate perfection. I felt so *sad*. I needed more. I told David about my ice cream tragedy and I asked him if he minded if we walked to the Giant in our neighborhood to see if they had any. He was amenable, so we went. Score! One more. We headed back to my place to put the ice cream away in the freezer. As we waited to cross the street I looked up at him and asked what he wanted to do next. Given that he was a 26 year old male, I was pretty sure I already knew what he wanted to do next. I did not want to do that though. Since he lived nearby and spoke Spanish, I wanted to keep him around. I thought if I *didn't* have sex with him on our first date I would be more likely to see him again. Isn't that what they say? So, before he could answer, I responded to my own question, "I know what *I* want to do! I want to grab my car and drive to the Giant off River Road. Wanna come?" Not what he expected. At this point he was probably confused as to how someone so normal looking could be so strange, although I *had* explained how much I LOVED this ice cream. But, he agreed to join. So, we went to another Giant. Fail. They had none left. However, I still wasn't ready to give up.

By this time, the sun had set and it was a beautiful summer night. The moon was full and it was *huge*. We looked at it together, glad that we were out and excited not to have missed it. We laughed about how atypical our date was as we drove to the *next* Giant. Fail again. Oh well. It was time to accept my ice cream cursed fate; at least I still had eleven pints in the freezer. After putting him through that wild goose chase, I felt obliged to share a pint with him, so that is what I did, outside, in the park, by the fountain, under the stars. I liked him a lot and was enjoying his company. I liked making out with him too once the ice cream was gone, the empty pint on the bench next to us. I liked his hands wandering over my body. Despite our very atypical date, it was a really, really nice night on planet earth with this strawberry blonde, perfectly bilingual stranger. I hoped I would see him again, speak Spanish with him again. I expected to. But, I never did.

He blew me off, ignored me. I didn't understand why he didn't even want to be friends. Though I did ask, he never explained why. Did he think I was crazy because I dragged him to three grocery stores? Was it because I didn't have sex with him? Who knows? The unkindness of being put in the position of wondering depresses me.

Sadly, David's name had to be added to my list of Guys Who are Not Nice. I keep this list because what else can you do when someone ignores you, ghosts on you, can't just properly reject you? Harassing them is pointless and will just make *you* look bad. They won't care anyway. So, I have the list and I write down their names. It makes me feel a little better but not better than I would feel if I didn't need the list at all.

31 Lists

I do keep a lot of lists. I started writing lists when I was a kid. I was inspired by Lois Lowry's *Anastasia* books. Anastasia was a little girl who loved to keep lists in her green notebook. I copied her, except my notebook was blue. I kept a list of the things I loved and the things I hated. Here is an excerpt from my love/hate list from middle school through high school:

Love: Art, creativity, good grades, imagination, flowers, beautiful things, Madonna, Roald Dahl, travelling, laugh attacks, gentlemen, cowboy hats, the beach, fairness, free stuff, being tan, trees, feeling good about myself, Spanish, getting awards, winning, watermelon, kissing, the earth, generosity, classical architecture

Hate: War, selfishness, self-centeredness, smoking, people who don't care, drugs, prejudice, sexist people, pollution, littering, dumb rules, liars, brushing my teeth with warm water, nuclear weapons, people who take things for granted, mosquitos, rude people, people who talk when I'm not done my test, getting woken up by a mosquito buzzing in my ear, racists, pop quizzes, killer bees, when my fingernails break, having vacations end, regrets, when people you love leave, drying off with damp towels, guys with long nails

I kept lists of my favorite names, movies, TV shows, flowers, authors, songs, the books I'd read, things I wanted, best days of my life, quotes, fears, personal traits. I kept a list of all the boys I loved. As I got older I kept a list of all the boys I kissed, then later, with whom I did more than kiss. I kept all sorts of lists in my Blue Notebook.

I still keep lists today but now my lists are digital. Of course, I have a list of all the people who have lived with me. Most of them have been good experiences. I have made great friends, got to visit some in foreign countries, was even a bridesmaid in one's beautiful destination wedding on Martha's Vineyard. But, not all have been great experiences. Number Six was extremely messy. So was Number 49. Number 54 accidentally broke a bunch of things. Number 37 was nice. Too nice. Suspiciously nice. No one is that nice. He helped me with chores, he watched TV with me, he was extremely nice and proper... until the day he disappeared and stiffed me for rent, leaving me with a vacant spot and no notice.

But, no one compared to Number Seventeen.

32 Roommate Number Seventeen

In her interview, Number Seventeen told me she doesn't "do drama." That was a red flag and I should have listened to my gut because I knew better. Seventy-one roommates to date and I have been right about every single one of them. I just didn't always listen to my instinct, as I should have with Number 37 and Number Seventeen. I knew they were bad news but I felt bad for them and I wanted to help them out. However, when someone tells you they don't "do drama," you can be pretty sure it means the exact opposite. Drama-free people don't need to make statements about drama; it doesn't cross their minds.

I liked Number Seventeen though. She was pretty and I am a sucker for a pretty face. She was tall, large, but very attractive. The policewoman said she was built "like a linebacker." Number Seventeen shared my room with me. She had a good sense of humor. She made me laugh despite the fact that something was off with her. I don't know the full extent of her story, but whatever it was caused her to be thirty something years old and living on an air mattress in someone else's bedroom. And, well, earning money in illegal ways. I just didn't know that at first.

There were four of us at that time. Chelsea and Emily shared the living room. I was thrilled with both of them, had a blast with them. Chelsea had one of the prettiest faces I'd ever seen up close. She was from Kentucky and came to DC to intern for her senator. She was wise beyond her years and had this perfect nose I just wanted to stare at all the time. I didn't want to make her uncomfortable, this 22 year old girl living with a 36 year old stranger, so I tried not to stare at her, at least not when she would notice.

It was winter when Chelsea moved in with me and that was back when I used to binge watch a lot of TV. At the time, I was watching *The L Word*, a show about lesbians written by writers who I swear hated their audience. Nothing you ever wanted to happen happened on that show, so you just rage-watched as you suffered through the series as quickly as possible in order to find out what happened to the characters you despised but in whom you were invested. Between me watching a show about lesbians and wanting to stare at her face, I was afraid Chelsea would get the wrong idea, but she was cool and settled right in with me and started rage-watching right along with me. How we hated Jenny Schecter! She was one of the most obnoxious TV villains we had ever encountered. If you want to truly hate a character, watch this show. Except don't, because then you will just rage-watch it too and wish you could get back the time you invested in suffering through six whole seasons.

This was in 2010, the year of the snowpocalypse in DC. Chelsea's and my work was cancelled for four days straight, followed by a weekend, as the city was shut down, crippled by the storm. Poor Number Seventeen and Emily did have to work so it was just Chelsea and me alone in the apartment every day for days on end. Waking up daily to a newly announced snow day? I hadn't enjoyed a winter that much since I was a kid! It was one of the best weeks of our lives, getting up when we woke up naturally, starting the day with *Wifeswap* and then hours and hours of *The L Word*, screaming at the TV when the characters did everything we did not want them to do and nothing that we did. A lifelong friendship was born in a blizzard, enhanced by a mutual hate for Jenny Schecter.

I just *loved* Chelsea. Since then she has come to Maine with me twice and I was a bridesmaid in her wedding. Chelsea with the quick wit, fantastic sense of humor, long brown hair, pretty blue eyes and perfect, perfect nose. Anytime Chelsea was doing something fun, she would proclaim, "This is the best day of my life!" I loved the funny voice she said it in and her extreme enthusiasm. I added it to my repertoire and now I often exclaim that I am having the best day of my life if I am happy and having fun. When you frame it that way, you can't even believe how many "best days" you get to have.

But, back to Number Seventeen. I got along with Number Seventeen but Number Seventeen did not get along with Emily and Chelsea. She was not friendly to them and she made them uncomfortable. She caused a negative vibe in the apartment. I considered it my job to provide a stress-free, comfortable environment for all the people who were paying me to live under my roof so I talked to her about it and she put in more of an effort to be less bristly and things did seem to improve. Until they got worse.

One day, I was at work and Emily and Chelsea were both home sick. Number Seventeen was supposed to be at work too but she came home early. With a man. She was not expecting to see Emily or Chelsea there. No one was happy about this surprise. As far as we knew, Number Seventeen did not have a boyfriend. This man was a stranger. In the middle of the day.

They told me about it but in my naiveté I brushed it off. Maybe she had met someone she liked but just hadn't told us? They told me they thought she was a prostitute. I was too innocent (and *actually* drama-free) to believe them. Things got more awkward. Though no one said anything, Number Seventeen knew her behavior was suspect and this caused her to become more antisocial. It got uncomfortable again. Very uncomfortable. Emily refused to keep living with her and moved out. I wasn't sure what to do. I did not want to lose Chelsea too.

James replaced Emily. At first James and Number Seventeen seemed to hit it off, but then he started to complain to me about her making him uncomfortable as well. Since it was soon after he had moved in, I knew that I liked him, but I still didn't *know* him. Throughout this whole time *I* still got along fine with Number Seventeen so I didn't know if I should believe what he was telling me about her or if he was trying to sabotage her for some reason. Things were so weird. I didn't know what to think! But, something was definitely going on. Chelsea started to look for a different place to live. I could *not* have that. I didn't know how to fix the situation but I knew that I needed to. And fast.

One day, James mentioned a conversation that he and Number Seventeen had had by text. I wanted to know if I could trust James because I needed to resolve the situation. So, when Number Seventeen was in the shower, I looked at her phone, easy to do since that was back in the day of flip phones, before locked screens. All I wanted to know was if what James had said was true. Had they had the texting conversation he had told me about? I was really not interested in invading her privacy. But, when I looked at her phone I saw all sorts of messages… from different men. And pricing. Pricing for sex acts. One I believe was called "tongue and thumb." Whatever that is.

Okay…

Breathe…

James was apparently telling the truth.

And Chelsea and Emily had apparently been right about Number Seventeen.

Apparently, Number Seventeen actually *was* a prostitute.

Oh boy.

You know, I didn't even care about how she earned her money. That was her deal. But, I minded that I was sharing my bedroom with someone who was a liar. And, someone who made my other roommates uncomfortable. And, who was making Chelsea think about moving out. And, who was causing a lot of *drama* in my apartment. She had to go.

I told Number Seventeen I needed her to move out by the first of the following month, in six weeks. She said no. She told me she was going to move out when *she* was ready. She refused to move out. And then she refused to talk to me. So, I was now sharing my room with a woman who was almost a foot taller than I am, who participated in illegal activity, who was ignoring me and basically holding my apartment hostage. I could not have that situation. I couldn't even sleep in my own room anymore. I started sleeping on the couch because I didn't know *what* she might do. It was awful. She was making everyone miserable by making our living situation so awkward, but I could tell she was very lonely and miserable herself and despite her behavior, I felt sorry for her.

I had always been extremely laid-back about how I rented out spots in my place. I needed help with my mortgage and I wanted to help people who needed a cheap place to live with a flexible commitment because housing in DC is very expensive and leases are often not very accommodating. I didn't charge them a security deposit. I didn't make them go through the hassle of signing a lease. Sometimes, if I remembered, or if someone requested, I'd provide a rental agreement. That was it. Now I was in a bad situation and I had to figure out what the law was, what my rights were, and how to get rid of this woman. I then learned that evicting someone is extremely difficult to do and can take months and months. That was not feasible. I did not know what to do. It was all so stressful I ended up losing seven pounds in one week.

And then a few days later, James couldn't find his keys. And I couldn't find some cash that I had. I couldn't take it anymore. So, I called the police. A policewoman came up to my apartment. I told her the situation. I didn't want to get Number Seventeen in trouble or have her arrested. I didn't even know for sure if she had taken these things. In fact, James did end up finding his keys and it turned out I had just misplaced the cash. I just wanted her out. I needed her *gone*. The policewoman looked at a picture of Number Seventeen, "She's built like a linebacker. She could crush you." It was scary. It was a scary situation.

Thank goodness for that policewoman. She advised me that I could get a restraining order and then Number Seventeen would not be allowed back in the apartment. I had a solution. James, still new to my apartment, barely knew me yet he saw the position I was in and became my most supportive friend. He accompanied me right then and there to the courthouse, taking an unpaid day off work to do so. I will never, ever forget his support that day. I will also never forget how when I treated James to pizza near the courthouse afterwards, he put *salt* on his pizza. Who *does* that?!

I filled out the paperwork and we had the hearing with the judge. I got my temporary restraining order. Number Seventeen would not be allowed back in the apartment. I went home and had the locks changed.

In the middle of the night, a policeman came to serve Number Seventeen her restraining order. But, she was not there. She actually never came back again, until months later to pick up her things, accompanied by the police. I don't know how it happened that the day I decided we couldn't take anymore was the day she decided she wasn't coming back. It just did.

Since we couldn't serve her the restraining order because we had no idea where she was, what I had was a temporary restraining order. Those are only good for one week and then they have to be renewed. I had to take time off from work and go back to that courthouse every single week to stand before a judge and ask for the order to be renewed for five weeks straight because, if I didn't have the order and she came back to the apartment, I would not have been allowed to not let her in. Finally, *finally* they found Number Seventeen in Michigan and finally were able to serve her the actual restraining order. I could *finally* forget about her.

I don't know whatever happened to Number Seventeen. Once I got on her bad side she was a scary bully so I was very glad she was gone, though I bear her no ill will. Thanks to her, I learned to never, ever not listen to my gut when considering allowing someone to live in my home and to definitely *never* rent to someone who says they "don't do drama."

February 2009 to fall 2017. Eight years. Seventy-one roommates. Mostly good memories. Some friends for life. The opportunity to receive help and to offer help. And miraculously, nothing missing or stolen, ever (except for a lot of tupperwares. Why do I have so many bottoms missing tops and vice versa?!). I am 43 years old and I have never lived by myself. I am ready to have my apartment to myself. But, I mean, I have 1,100 square feet. It seems kind of selfish to have all that space just for me.

In my blue notebook there is a When I Grow Up list and

on it is "I want to throw lots of fancy parties." I would like to implement that already but it is hard when you have mattresses in your living room. Someday.

33 My Bad Date Story

One person who will not have an invitation to any fancy party I might have is Connor. Oh, Connor. Connor was my worst Bumble date.

I am a very friendly and outgoing person so unlike other people I have talked to, I am never hesitant to meet someone or apprehensive that I will be bored or not have any fun on a first date. I had never worried about wondering "how to get out of it" if it wasn't going well. I usually always at least have a mildly pleasant time on dates. So, I assumed that would be the case when Connor asked me to meet him at an Irish bar downtown. I had never been there before and one of the things I like about dating is when the guy picks the place and I get to go somewhere new. I got there first and quickly confirmed the fact that Irish bars are *not* my scene. At all. Oh well.

Then, Connor walked in and my dislike for him was immediate. I did not like his face. It wasn't that he didn't look like his photos. He did. I wasn't thrilled with the photos of his face either, but I thought maybe they didn't do him justice. They did. It wasn't that he was ugly, I just Did. Not. Like. His. Face. At all. And I just did not like *him*. He sat down at the bar with me and I thought, for the first time ever, "HOW AM I GOING TO GET OUT OF THIS??!" He ordered a club soda. I ordered an ice water. I don't know why he asked me to meet him at a bar. I just wanted to leave but I didn't know how. Also, given that I had paid for my transportation to get there, I was determined to not have my metro fare go to waste. I was *going* to have a good time, gosh darn it!

Connor was not a great conversationalist so I threw out some topics to get us talking while he kept staring at me. It wasn't a smoldering gaze. It was a stare, a stare in which I think he was probably trying to picture me naked and trying to be obvious about it. It wasn't sexy. At all. Luckily, my tolerance for awkward is high.

"You know you have a very intense gaze?" I asked.

"Uh, eh, um, do I? Uh, sorry." He fumbled.

It was better after that, at least he stopped staring at me. I found some topics and we actually did end up having a nice enough conversation. Things seemed to be improving. Except his face. That stayed the same.

Since the conversation had started to flow less painfully, when he asked me if I would like to go for a walk, I said, "Sure." I am always up for going for a walk anyway and if I was going to be hanging out with someone whose face I didn't like, at least I would be burning some calories. As soon as I said yes, he basically jumped off his stool, threw on his coat and looked like he was about to walk out right then and there.

"Um, don't you have to pay?" I asked.

"Uh, eh, um… I only got a club soda." He fumbled again.

"Um, yeah, but don't you have to *pay* for it?"

"Oh, um, yeah, I, um, yeah… I didn't realize. I wasn't thinking. It's not like I was trying to be a Jew and walk out without paying."

WHATTTTTTTTTTT??????????

I could not believe he said that out loud. I was shocked.

I looked straight at him and said, "Well, I am Jewish and that is so offensive and I just want to cry right now that you just said that to me."

He looked mortified and said, "Um, I'm sorry! I didn't mean it! It is just like calling someone a sand n… um, it's just like saying the N word."

WHATTTTTTTTTTT?????????

"Do you SAY THE N WORD?!?!?!!"

His response? "Yeah, it's just like calling someone a fag who isn't gay."

Wow.

By this time my jaw was practically on the floor. I couldn't believe that people still talked this way! In public! To strangers! On dates!

I was appalled.

I excused myself to go to the bathroom. I needed to collect my thoughts and figure out how to extricate myself gracefully from this situation, as the lady I aspire to be. I figured that since the guy was clearly an anti-Semite, a racist, and a homophobe, he was probably a misogynist too and I didn't want to give him something else to add to his narrative. I also believe in leading by example and being a good representative for my gender so I needed to think of a way to end the date firmly and directly but with poise.

Well, if you think of something that meets those requirements in this type of situation, let me know because... I had nothing.

Luckily for me, by the time I got out of the bathroom, he was long gone.

So yeah, Connor will definitely NOT be receiving an invitation to any fancy parties I hope to have. No WAY.

I do love to entertain. I love to have people over. I love to have parties and especially dinner parties. I put the beds away and I make the apartment look pretty with lots of fresh flowers and candles. I love to plan a menu, figure out the logistics of when each item needs to be prepped and/or cooked so that everything will be ready at the same time. I love to have friends around the dining room table, talking and laughing, telling stories or talking politics. When I moved to DC, I envisioned a life of endless dinner parties in beautiful homes. However, I never ended up meeting the people with the beautiful homes and it seems that no one ever has dinner parties anymore. But, despite my air mattresses in my living room, I do.

When I was married, Alejandro would be in charge of the beverages. Since I barely drink alcohol and don't drink soda or coffee or tea or really anything other than water and milk, beverages are not my forté. They are just not something I am good at. I miss having someone help me with the beverages. I would like someone for that. And someone to be proud of me for how I gracefully prepare and host a party and convene a diverse group of interesting, intelligent, funny, and attractive people (clearly not Connor's scene). But, I don't have that. So, I am just bad at beverages.

Another thing I am bad at is buying socks. I used to be okay at buying socks so I don't know if it is truly that I am bad at it or that the sock selection has changed. I just can't seem to find socks that I like anymore so most of my socks have holes. I really need new socks. Badly.

34 Yep. That happened.

Mastro's is a steakhouse downtown where they have live music every night in the bar. I go there often because there are these two singers who I just absolutely love to see. Jeremy and Julia are so unbelievably talented - I always say that Julia sings Adele better than Adele and Jeremy can basically sing ANYTHING. I have become friends with them both and I stress over Julia's career. I stress that she will get famous and I won't be able to sit at the piano and practically have her all to myself and I stress that she isn't *already* famous and that America is being deprived of her talent. It is basically a national tragedy. It is also a national tragedy that Jeremy is not famous but since that isn't a goal of his, I luckily do not have to stress over his career. I have been to this place so many times and have brought so many different people to see Jeremy and Julia that the restaurant really should pay me a commission.

I have a lot of male friends that I have brought to Mastro's on friend dates, to the point where I was starting to worry that the bartenders and wait-staff were going to think I was an escort. I told this to my friend Bayo as we arrived there one time and mentioned that hopefully they didn't really think that since when I go with my male friends I still pay for myself. And then, when the check came, being the generous gentleman that he is, Bayo paid for me. Oh well. So what if they thought that I was a hooker? The talent was not to be missed and the food is great.

One night, I was there with my friend Tanya. We were sitting at my regular table in the bar, enjoying each other's company and swooning over Jeremy and Julia's talent when all of a sudden, this handsome man walked by on his way to the bathroom. We caught each other's gaze and held it. I was shocked as I never, ever find someone handsome who is also age appropriate. But he *was* age appropriate *and* he was handsome. Very.

I told Tanya that when he walked by on his way back, I was going to say hi to him. But, he was less bold on his return trip and did not look at me and did not hear me when I said hi. Oh well.

About an hour later he walked by again, this time with his friend. He *looked* at me again. I *looked* at him right back. There was no way he was going to get away a second time. I told Tanya I was going to try again this time, louder. When he walked back, I leaned way over and said "Are you going to keep walking by me without saying hi or what?" And that was that. He came over and we introduced ourselves. Mark with the very blonde hair and the very blue eyes and the movie star good looks, a DC Daniel Craig. I could feel his energy right away and I liked the way it felt. He said he would come over with his friends when they were done with dinner and join us. It was so exciting.

Shortly after, the waitress came over with two glasses of champagne that *he had sent to our table.* That was so cool! So classy! I was thrilled. Despite the fact that I don't like alcohol and I don't like carbonated beverages, I'd always loved the idea of a man sending a drink to my table. That was a dream come true!

He and his friends joined us when they finished their meal. It was getting late, so Tanya excused herself and headed home. So there I was, the woman who can't seem to date anyone over 37 with three real, live grown-up men. Everyone had high energy, friendliness level on max. It was a blast to be fun and flirty and confident. Mark's friends kept raving about his condo and his rooftop so, after we shut the place down, when he invited me to come home with him and see it, my curiosity had been piqued and I couldn't resist. I felt pretty confident I'd be safe. He was a prominent businessman with a fair amount of Google results so I wasn't nervous. Yes, of course I googled him right then and there in front of them.

Well.

They were not kidding. His apartment was 4,500 square feet, overlooking the Potomac. Selena Gomez played on the stereo system throughout the whole home as we talked and flirted and made out in his beautiful modern day palace which also, by the way, was featured in *Home & Design* magazine, a copy of which he offered me and I absolutely and shamelessly accepted so I could show all my friends. I could not even believe I was in such a fancy home. Was this my life? Handsome stranger I meet at an upscale restaurant, champagne sent to my table, now hanging out in a giant, gorgeous apartment? Pinch me. I couldn't believe this was really happening. Things became a bit more intimate.

He led me over to the bed, the perfectly made king size bed with the perfect, probably 1,000 thread count bedding. Was I really in such a fancy place? He kissed me and then he bent down to take off my shoes. And there I am in this beautiful, multimillion dollar, professionally decorated, everything perfect apartment…

…with my socks full of holes.

Yep. That happened.

I told you - I really need new socks!

We did have one official date after that; I guess my socks didn't scare him off. He picked me up at my apartment in his new car to take me out to dinner at Mastro's again. His new car: a Ferrari FF. Do you know that those start at $295,000? That car was worth almost as much as my apartment where I had two people living in my living room!

I've never been one to be impressed by fancy cars though. I have no interest in cars. The only kind of cars I like are Jeeps and preferably the older, boxier models. I don't like the new curvy ones. I have a Jeep; Alejandro and I bought it together. It was the first and only car I have ever owned, bought when I was 28 years old. We paid $4,800 in cash. I've never had a car payment. It doesn't have power locks or windows, air conditioning or a radio. It is even missing a back passenger window that I never fixed after a cyclist crashed into me and put his head through it. I would love a newer Jeep, but I don't understand the point of getting rid of a car that works. So, I will keep it until it doesn't work anymore.

35 I learned to drive a stick shift in France.

Despite my lack of interest in cars, I *have* been around a lot of fancy ones. After I graduated from college I became an au pair in France. I was placed with a family in the south of France in a little town called Mouans-Sartoux, just a few miles outside of Cannes. While living there, I learned to recognize Ferraris and Bentleys and Rolls Royces. I had my own little car while I lived with this family, a little red Renault Cinq. Not fancy by any means, but it got me and the daughters I chauffeured around. Since the daughters were thirteen and eleven, my main task with them as their au pair was to drive them places. That meant I needed to learn to drive a stick shift. Nicole, the mother, told me, "We really like you, but if you can't learn to drive stick, we can't keep you." No pressure. She arranged for a private instructor to come and teach me. Good thing I work well under pressure because I did learn to drive a stick shift. In French. In an incredibly hilly place.

The family lived up a very, very steep hill and it was quite a feat learning to get up there without rolling down. I am not even going to pretend that that was fun. It was not. But, I was in love with the family from the first moment I saw beautiful, elegant, blonde Nicole at the train station and prayed, "Please let her be my host mother."[1] So, I needed to learn because I needed to stay.

My sojourn with this wonderful French family started with a train ride from Paris to Cannes. As I wrote in a letter to my parents:

> I looked out the window the whole time and got to see six hours of beautiful countryside and farmland. The further south we got, the more hilly and mountainous it got and then all of a sudden, we were riding along the Mediterranean!

That was the first time I had seen the Mediterranean; my parents had never seen it. I wish I could remember that moment, but it is lost. I am so glad my parents saved my letters, so at least it is captured on paper.

I had never packed for living abroad before; I didn't know how one even did that. I figured I had to bring *everything* so I packed in the biggest type of bag I knew of – a hockey bag. Two of them,

[1] This was before Facebook so I had no idea what she looked like!

actually. Do you know how heavy a fully stuffed hockey bag is? *Heavy*. I think each one weighed 80 pounds. I don't know what I was thinking.

As I continued in the letter to my parents:

> I was really worried about getting my luggage off the train in time and then getting it from the train station to the car! But again, I was *lucky* and this man *carried* my hockey bags for me! He was travelling with his very pregnant wife who waited by the second bag on the platform while he brought out the first bag. I waited in the station with the first bag and all my other luggage as he went back and forth to retrieve their bags and my second bag. I kept seeing this really pretty and extremely well-dressed blonde lady walk by and I was hoping she was my host mother. She knew I had a ton of bags, so when she saw my huge bag down with the man's wife, she thought maybe that was me so she approached her and then saw that she was pregnant and was like, "Oh no! What are we getting ourselves into??" She asked her, "Are you Jennifer?" And the lady said, "No, but I know who Jennifer is!"

After Nicole finally found me and the nice man loaded my huge hockey bags into her little Mercedes convertible, we laughed about that all the way home. Our incredibly close and affectionate relationship as host mother and daughter, as well as friends and confidants, started out with mistaken identity and shared laughter.

The family lived in a beautiful house full of antique furniture and paintings of trompe l'oeils. I don't think I had ever seen a Venetian chandelier before, but that was what hung over their dining room table and, therefore, meant I definitely needed to have a Venetian chandelier some day in my own dining room (I do. Venetian chandelier hanging from the ceiling, air mattresses on the floor). I loved it and I loved everything about that house. The house was on the side of that steep hill I had to learn to drive up, overlooking the town below. That was where I also learned that houses should have a view.

The light pink, stucco house with terra cotta roof encircled the swimming pool, every room looking out onto it. Downstairs, first was the kitchen, then the dining room, then the living room, then the guest bedroom, then the parents' room. All of these rooms had sliding glass doors that retracted into the walls so that there would be no barrier between the inside of the house and the outside patio. The girls' bedrooms were upstairs, each overlooking the pool as well and each had its own terrace. You could never be bored in that house because of that view. The view of the patio, the pool, the sky, palm trees, olive groves and the town below. You could watch the clouds roll by all day or, on cloudless days, you could observe the clear blue change color as the day progressed from morning to afternoon to evening. It was a perfect Provençal house. I loved it.

There were always fresh flowers on the coffee table in the living room, usually a big bouquet of ranunculus that Nicole would buy each week at the marché. Of course, that is where I learned that ranunculus are my favorite flowers. Sometime in late February/early March when the mimosa trees bloom, Manuel, the father, came home with his arms full of bouquets of those bright yellow flowers for all the ladies of the household, including me. They smelled sweet and it was such a sweet gesture. He always made me feel included.

They treated me like I was part of the family. Berenice, the thirteen year old with a serious attitude, and I would argue like we were sisters. I learned to fight in French! Melanie, the adorable and affectionate eleven year old gave me lots of hugs and hung out with me when she wasn't busy with friends her own age.

I had my own little cabin, down the hill from the main house and on the other side of a little olive grove. At night, at bedtime, when it was time for me to go "home," I would walk through that olive grove, under the stars, accompanied by fireflies flurrying about and happy thoughts, anxious to go to sleep, so I could get up in the morning and have another perfect day in a perfect place with people I loved.

The house had four refrigerators, one in the laundry room, one in the kitchen and two in the garage. Manuel was a produce wholesaler so every week he would come home with a car full of the most delicious, fresh vegetables and fruits, including exotic fruits like litchi nuts and passion fruit. I was introduced to them both there, and I loved them. Whenever I get to have passion fruit anything now, it always reminds me of my time with my French family.

Every day would start off with fresh-squeezed orange juice (one of my responsibilities). Most meals were prepared by Fatima, their lovely Tunisian housekeeper. I spent a lot of time in the kitchen with Fatima but stupidly did not pay attention to how she made the wonderful meals she prepared (one of the biggest regrets of my life). Nicole was also an excellent cook and made the best lasagna I have ever had, lasagna with béchamel instead of ricotta. I have never been able to replicate it myself, but I did figure out how to make Fatima's delicious ratatouille. Other common meals included rabbit pot roast (I learned that rabbit tastes like chicken), baked potatoes with caviar (I cannot believe how much caviar I got to eat with this family; I was so spoiled), fondue served with bread and potatoes for dipping (yes, I gained a ton of weight), and my favorite, Nicole's homemade pâté de foie gras. Oh. My. God. I could not get enough of that. Dinner was always at least three courses, the main course, the salad course, and then the cheese course. Manuel loved his camembert at the end of every meal.

They included me in their meals at home and also took me out to nice restaurants with them. On Sundays we would have brunch at the country club where they played golf. They were lovely people. Friendly, warm, wealthy but not pretentious. Kind. Nicole and I both have birthdays in January and for our birthdays they took us to the circus... in *Monaco*. It was a small, intimate little circus. Having been fascinated by that tiny country ever since I was little, it was a dream come true and even more so when I noticed that we were sitting a few rows back from Prince Rainier and Princess Caroline. Was I really at the circus in *Monaco* with members of the Monegasque *royal family*? Was this my life? It felt like a dream.

Scott, my college boyfriend, came to visit me and the family welcomed him just as they had welcomed me. One night, when Nicole and the girls were away for the weekend, Manuel took the two of us out to dinner in St. Paul de Vence, a medieval hilltop town which looks down on the Mediterranean from one side and up at the Alps from the other. I don't know what compelled Manuel to be so generous as take us to eat at La Colombe d'Or, a gem of a restaurant, but I am so grateful to him for giving us this memory of this place that we otherwise wouldn't even have known existed.

La Colombe d'Or was founded as an inn and restaurant in 1920 and became a haven for artists who would often pay for their meals and lodging with their art. Back then, they were just artists; today they are known as world famous masters. There I was, a 23 year old American, living in the South of France, dining in the most beautiful restaurant I had ever seen, surrounded by original works of Picasso, Matisse, Léger, Chagall, Calder, and Braque. On top of that, Belinda Carlisle, top 10 recording artist, was seated a few tables away from us as we munched on our basket of crudité, presented as if it had just been picked from the garden. I felt like the luckiest girl in the world.

Those were very happy times. I loved this family, even difficult Berenice, and I didn't ever want to not be with them, so I didn't really make many friends of my own or go out like normal 23 year olds. I had no interest in nightlife or partying. I've never been that way; as I've said, I prefer family time. At night we would sit around and play cards or Yam, a kind of game you play with dice. You can play Yam with others, or you can play by yourself and it is *very* addictive. As I wrote in my journal:

> First of all, about 1-2 months ago, Yam found its way into our home. First we were a happy family that spent quality time together after dinner, but then they started playing Yam. And that was the end of our happy family. Every single night, they played. And, when Melanie came home from school, the first words out of her mouth would be "Tu veux jouer un Yam avec moi, Maman?" [*Do you want to play Yam with me, Mom?*] The sound of dice rolling has not ceased in the house. Manuel is so mental about the game that no one is allowed to talk to him while he's playing and if you're playing with him and your mind isn't 100% on the game, watch out. I hated the game. Just hearing the word "Yam" made me cringe. But then Scott came and we caught the fever. The reason why I am writing this is because the proof of how addicting it is is pretty funny. This morning before I had to go get my parents at the airport, I started playing and I was getting the best rolls. So, I couldn't stop! And, after not seeing my parents for *six months*, I was late picking them up from the airport because of Yam!

My parents came to visit me for a week. Again, the family welcomed my company as if they were their own. And what did my French family give my parents as a parting gift when they left? A Yam set to take back to the States!

We all sat around the table together for many meals during my parents' stay, either at home or at restaurants, me serving as translator. For one such meal, Nicole prepared a *feast*: veal accompanied by roasted red peppers and roasted garlic, potato gratin, ratatouille, followed by the salad course, the cheese course, and then fresh strawberries and a fruit tarte for dessert. To accompany the meal, Manuel selected both red and white wines from his wine cellar which my dad enthusiastically enjoyed (both the fact that Manuel had a wine cellar and the wines themselves).

My parents stayed in my little cabin with me. While they were there, we toured the Côte d'Azure visiting the little towns along the way to Monaco and then Italy. The drive to Italy was 100 kilometers, about sixty miles. Being so close to Italy, I had made the drive various times with my little Renault Cinq. It was so cool to me that I could just drive from one country to the next. On the drive with my parents I thought, "I bet I could do this on my bike. I am going to try it!" I had always loved bike riding and I already had bought a bike which I rode downhill to Cannes most days to go to the beach and then uphill to go back home. It was a good workout and a good way to avoid dealing with beach parking.

My daily bike rides became my training - every day down to Cannes and back up to Mouans-Sartoux. I can't remember how long I trained for but it was long enough for me to feel confident that I could make the trek to Italy. Finally, one morning I got up at 5 AM and I set out. I rode and I rode. I rode in bike shorts and a bikini top, and when I'd get hot I'd just stop and take a swim in the Mediterranean. I took my time, riding through Juan Les Pins, Antibes, Nice, Monaco, Menton, stopping at different beaches, taking lots of photos. I made it to Ventimiglia, Italy, the first town on the Italian side. I was proud of myself. I had set a goal, trained for it and achieved it. I felt strong, capable, independent. I even did it a second time, riding further into Italy to San Remo. I felt like I could do anything. Those were good feelings.

I didn't smell good though. Not at all. Sneakers that have been in an out of the Mediterranean and wet all day acquire quite a stench. Riding the train back to Cannes was embarrassing. I felt bad for the people around me. Oh well.

Aside from riding my bike, playing yam, staring out the windows at the view, going to the beach and just spending time with the family, a large amount of my leisure time was spent on correspondence. I wrote pages and pages and PAGES of letters to friends and family while I was there. Manuel photocopied all my letters for me at his office so that I could keep a record of my words and memories. Sometimes I would write at night at my little desk in my little cabin, other times I would write from the terrace of the outdoor dining room of the house, overlooking the valley below, sometimes, as I wrote in a letter to Angela, my best friend from college:

I'm in Cannes, writing you from the famous Croissette, the boulevard which runs along the beach. Everyone is out promenading. I'm sitting on a chair overlooking the beach and the Mediterranean.

How lucky was I?

I am so grateful to have these letters and my journal from this special time in my life. So many of my memories have faded, but all that painstaking writing was a gift from my past self that enables me to go back to that time through my written accounts.

They say you don't remember so much what people do or say, you remember how they made you feel, and if there is one thing that I do remember from my time in France, without needing it in writing, it is that I felt loved and included by this wonderful family who treated me as their own.

36 Vous êtes trop beau!

My time in Mouans-Sartoux overlapped with the Cannes film festival. That is where I met Gille. Berenice and her friend wanted me to drive them to Cannes and drop them off so they could look for celebrities. There was a ton of traffic on the narrow streets and the sidewalks were very crowded. All of a sudden, I saw him - the most attractive guy I had seen since I had been in France. Actually, one of the most attractive males I had seen, ever. Since we were driving at a snail's pace, I saw I caught his eye as well, so I shouted to him out the window, "Vous êtes trop beau!" *You are too handsome!* He flashed me a big smile and said thank you. I told the girls, "I am GOING to find him again." Given the size of the crowd, I knew that would be difficult but I was determined! I dropped off the girls and then found a place to park, thinking I would see if I could sight any celebrities myself while I searched for the handsome Frenchman. I actually did - I saw a whole bunch: Bruce Willis, Demi Moore, Woody Harrelson, Steven Spielberg and the beautiful French actress Emmanuelle Béart, who stepped out of her limo right in front of me.

But, more exciting than those celebrity sightings was that I found the handsome Frenchman again! I don't know how we managed that, but we did. I told him again how handsome I thought he was - Gille with the perfectly symmetrical face, brown hair, a few days of scruff, light brown eyes and muscular body. I wondered what it felt like to be so attractive. He told me he thought I was pretty. I thought he was wayyyyyyy better looking than I was so I was surprised he even wanted to talk to me. But, he did. I saw that he was wearing a Jewish star around his neck, so I pulled out the tiny one I had around mine that I have worn since I was a little girl and we delighted in our surprise that we already had something in common. We liked each other right away and he ditched his friends to hang out with me, which was very flattering. We walked up and down the Croisette together, oblivious to the crowds, to the celebrities, to the paparazzi camera flashes, to the limos and to the Mediterranean. We walked and talked, back and forth, back and forth, getting to know each other, until it was time for me to meet the girls and drive them home, after which I promised to come right back so that we could find each other again. This time, we set a meeting place, but without cell phones we had to trust each other that we would both show up.

I drove back to Mouans-Sartoux to drop off Berenice and her friend as fast as I could and then I sped back to our meeting place in Cannes where we (miraculously) found each other once again. I joined him and his friends for a very late dinner and didn't get back home until 5 o'clock in the morning! He was so nice and polite, friendly and cool. I really liked him!

This was before anyone I knew had a cell phone or email. He wasn't going to be able to text me or friend me or snap me or call me, unless it was on the landline at the house. I gave him my number and he said he would call me the next day so that we could see each other again before he went back to Paris, where he was from. He was staying in Juan les Pins, one town over from Cannes, for a few days at an apartment his family owned. We had such a nice time together, so I was pretty confident that I would hear from him. But, you never know with these things. I wasn't looking forward to the dreaded anxiety-ridden waiting-by-the-phone. The next day I planted myself in the kitchen, next to the phone, ready to begin what I hoped would not be a long vigil. I warned everyone that they better stay off the phone, especially Berenice! As promised, he did call, before too much anxiety or suffering occurred and so I got to add Love Affair with a Handsome Frenchman to my list of experiences while living in France. We really did have a nice little love affair.

He was supposed to just be in town until that Saturday but he changed his ticket so that he could be with me until Tuesday! We spent time together in Mouans-Sartoux and Cannes and Juan Les Pins. As usual, my host family, treating me as if I really were one of them, had him over for a family dinner one night.

And then, Gille had to go back to Paris. He said we could call and write, but I didn't expect him to do it. Well, guess who called me as soon as he got home? Yes, he did! *And* he wrote me letters. We ended up talking on the phone one to two times a week! He wanted to come back to visit me again but when he wasn't able to, do you know what my host family did? They *gave* me a plane ticket and told me to go have a weekend in Paris with Gille. I got to go visit my French amour in *Paris* for a weekend, which may or may not have included being made love to on the hood of his car in his driveway. In *Paris*. I really couldn't believe this was my life; yet again, I felt like I was in a movie.

After I got back from Paris, Nicole told me the family was going to be going away for an upcoming weekend and suggested I have Gille come back to visit so I wouldn't be alone. Luckily, he was able to, and we got to spend more time together and have their beautiful house all to ourselves. I was just overwhelmed by their kindness, generosity, warmth and support.

I spent my last few days in France with Gille as well, since I was flying back to the States from Paris. After I came back to the States, we continued to write each other letters. And then, he even came to visit me in Maine! So, our little love affair became an international one. I knew I couldn't get attached to him so I enjoyed my time with him for what it was and what it could be, nothing more than a lovely, extended moment with another human being on planet earth.

This concept of just enjoying a moment on earth was introduced to me by Nicole, through the music of Francis Cabrel. France's version of James Taylor often played on the Bang and Olufsen throughout the house when we were home. I loved his music and his songs touched me, despite not being able to fully understand most of them. One song impacted me with its achingly poetic and beautiful lyrics and those lyrics embedded themselves deep within my subconscious and became part of me, forming my outlook toward moments, serving me twenty years later as I navigated the dating world where moments are often all I have. "Samedi Soir Sur La Terre" *Saturday evening on Earth* is about a man and a women who meet in a bar. They catch each other's eye, sparks fly, and the beginning of a love affair ensues.

But, it is the chorus that made an impression on me; he sings that this is a common story, just simply a Saturday evening on earth.

> Une histoire ordinaire
> On est tout simplement, simplement
> Un samedi soir sur la terre.

I loved the idea of viewing a Saturday evening not just as a Saturday evening, but a Saturday evening on planet earth. We are here just momentarily; the earth continues its orbit regardless of what we do or what is happening in our lives. If we think of our lives in the bigger picture of moments on earth, those moments can seem either more inconsequential or more remarkable, depending on which serves our emotional perspective. We can remind ourselves that the bad moments will soon pass. And the good ones? We must consciously, fully embrace them, while at the same time we are wishing we could prolong them. That way, after those good moments have passed, when we think about them, we can be even more grateful that we lived them and were able to experience them and that we are here, that we exist, as the earth continues to spin on its axis, hurling us through space and time.

37 Moments

When I was growing up I thought about things in terms of the long-term; I wanted that relationship that would last a lifetime. Fast forward to the current dating world and people are constantly appearing in and disappearing from your life so fast it can make your head spin. You might have a great time with someone and you think for sure you will have a second date and then they just disappear and you never hear from them or see them again.

Because of this, I have learned to be hyper aware of moments. If I am having fun, I want to pause, take it in, close my eyes, feel my consciousness absorb every aspect, hopefully capture a memory: Ben in my kitchen preparing fish tacos for us with sea bass that he caught himself, Seth walking me home and feeling how nice my hand felt in his, walking around London with Danny, making out like teenagers on every street corner (well, he was a teenager!), taking a break from hiking with Paul to eat the picnic he prepared for us, every second I had with Nathan. Those were all moments to be treasured as they happened. I soaked in every look, word spoken, felt the energy. I focused. I can't look back and say, "Oh, I wish I had enjoyed more or paid better attention" because I made the conscious effort to do it as I was living it. I might not have the lifetime love I wanted, but I have amassed a collection of moments.

Sometimes it is hard not to feel sorry for myself that moments seem to be all I have. Some of them I wanted to last so much longer. I definitely would have liked more moments with Ben who couldn't keep his hands off me and felt like a soulmate as he made me laugh. I would have liked more moments with Paul who had piercing eye contact and whose energy had a chemical reaction in my own body, making me feel energy in every cell, his vibe making me high as a kite. I would have definitely liked more of that. Or the utter peace and tranquility and calmness I felt in Nathan's presence? I would have liked that for a lifetime.

38 Eric

I don't know how to describe what I have with Eric, Eric with the buzz cut, the green eyes, and the long eyelashes. He is not my boyfriend but he is not a Not Boyfriend. Is he my friend with benefits? I don't know if that is appropriate either. Maybe he is. I take the word "friend" very seriously and I don't know if I would categorize him as that. I think I am more his friend than he is mine. I am usually the one to reach out and ask how he is doing.

He rarely asks about me, as a true friend would. Maybe he is my companion with benefits? But that sounds so awkward.

I feel very comfortable with Eric. Maybe it is because he is also from Maine. I felt a kinship with him right from the beginning. He grew up one town over from me. He knows where I come from. That means something to me as I don't date a lot of men in my own demographic. Since I rarely go out with people my own age, I don't have a lot of generational overlap, and I have dated very few other Jewish people so I haven't had much ethnic overlap. My ex-husband was a Catholic from Argentina and my last boyfriend was an Arab Muslim from Jordan so there were NO religious or ethnic or cultural overlaps. Eric is also twelve years younger than me so we don't share an age demographic either but there is a comfort in at least having a shared geographic background. He knows the Old Port and about greenhead flies and winters in Maine and having a variety of sleds from which to choose.

I suppose Eric is on the Roster but when I see him, he also actually hangs out with me. We go for walks and he holds my hand. We don't intertwine our fingers, he just holds my hand in his. It reminds me of when I was little and my parents used to hold my hand. It feels safe and secure even though our palms do get sweaty after a bit. But, I don't like to let go, even with sweaty palms. It feels nice to have my hand in someone else's, to have male companionship. On these walks, Eric talks my ear off about his job or the latest podcast he listened to or about politics. He is interesting so I like to listen to all the things he talks about. I try to focus on what he is saying but sometimes I really just close my eyes and think about how nice it feels to have my hand in his, the fact that a man is holding my hand. It is nice to cuddle up on the couch with him and watch a movie, put my head on his shoulder and be grateful for his masculine presence. When Eric comes to see me he always spends the night. Having him in my bed is a nice respite from being alone so I like that he stays with me.

Eric spent this past Christmas Eve and Christmas with me. He didn't have his son this year so he was going to be very lonely as well, a single dad and a lonely Jew both far from their families in Maine. We cooked together and watched movies and went for walks and I was so grateful to have his company and to not be alone on this loneliest day of the year when you can't go on Facebook because you will see pictures of everyone celebrating with their families and you feel even lonelier, not only because you don't have that but also because you wonder why no one ever invites you to join them.

Eric and I have not defined whatever this Not Relationship is. We haven't talked about it. I don't feel compelled to. He is focused on his career and his son and he doesn't have much else to offer me other than his companionship once in a while. I have learned to not want something from someone that they don't have to offer, so I just enjoy Eric's company when I have it, tell him I appreciate his companionship, don't get attached, and just savor the moment.

39 What You Know When You Are from Maine

I like to say that being born in Maine was the best thing I ever did. Of course I had no say in the matter, but I like the way it sounds. And it is the truth.

Maine.

When you grow up in Maine you know a lot of things worth knowing. You know about nature and seasons and neighborliness, friendship, recycling, and small town life. You know about the ocean and the sky and the stars and how to spot rainbows. These are all good things to know and they help you keep your perspective when you live in a place where you feel removed from nature and you come to know a lot of things you are not necessarily better off knowing.

In the winter, when you grow up in Maine, you have a variety of sleds to choose from and you spend hours sledding down your backyard hill, giving turns to each sled. You learn in the woods that if you bury yourself under the snow, it insulates you and keeps you warm. You lay your head back and look up at the snow covered trees and the grey sky and you listen to the silence.

Sometimes it is below zero while you wait for the school bus. It is too cold to walk to school and too cold to stand outside where you are supposed to wait. You have anxiety that you will miss the bus because you are not where you are supposed to be. You never do miss it though. Your mom helps you watch for it out the window and despite the cold, your memories are warm and secure.

You have a space heater in your room, a little old electric one that you know how to turn on by yourself. It is hard to get out of bed in the winter. The house is freezing. You get up the nerve and jump out of bed and turn on the heater and watch the coils start to glow orange. You have to dress right in front of that heater because just a few inches from it the room is still freezing.

Your dad teaches you how to ice skate on the pond down the street. When you fall down he says, "Why are you sitting?" After you have learned to skate, you spend hours and hours and hours skating at Joanna's pond with her brothers and sister. You can't feel your toes but you can't stop; it is too much fun. When it is time to go in, Susan, their mother, has hot chocolate ready for you. Each mug has two packs of Swiss Miss instead of one and you learn that *this* is the way to make hot chocolate.

In the spring you have the forsythia and the lilacs and the

crocuses and the rhododendrons that bloom. The lilacs on the side of the house are purple, the ones in the backyard are white. You know that there are daffodils that bloom right by the rhododendrons at the edge of the woods. There are just two or three of them and they have ruffled petals, unlike any daffodils you have seen anywhere else. You wonder how they ended up there in that spot. There is an area of the yard by the bulkhead where violets grow. You pick bouquets of violets and put them in a tiny vase in your room. You know that on the side of the house, behind the forsythia bush there is a patch of moss. You know that moss only grows in the shade and that it is soft. You like to sit down next to it and pet it for a little while, taking a break from your rounds of the yard.

Sometimes, if you are lucky, you might find a little toad hopping around the front yard and if you are really lucky, you can catch it. They aren't hard to catch, actually. He'll let you hold him for a little while and you will look at his spotted skin and little eyes until he pees on you and you screech and let him go. You know that caterpillars are soft and fuzzy and you love to catch those as well and let them crawl on your arms.

Your backyard is big and the grass has never been cut so dandelions and wildflowers grow there. It is so pretty - until one day it gets mowed and it never grows back the same and this is the worst tragedy of your childhood.

There is a beautiful, symmetrical tree in the backyard that you are able to climb up and on whose first branch you sit. From your perch in that tree you observe the yard, under that canopy of blossoming green, deciding where to explore next.

You are allowed to walk around the Old Port by yourself because Portland is a safe city. Your mom drops you off with your allowance in your pocket and you walk along the cobblestone streets, stopping in all your favorite stores. They are not chain stores; but are individually owned businesses. This matters to you as you grow up and you see that wherever you visit it is always the same because of the chain stores. But, Portland remains unique and you are grateful for that. You take yourself out to lunch at Allan's Incredible Edibles. You sit at the counter and order a cheeseburger. You feel independent and you are, even though you are still a kid.

In the summer, because you are very lucky, you move to your summer house. It is just twenty minutes away, on the coast. You have a big front porch where you have breakfast in the morning while you watch the traffic and the people heading to the beach. Everyone is an early bird because Maine is in the wrong time zone and the sun has already been up for hours by 7 AM. That is not too early to go to the beach and take a walk or lay in the sun. You know all your neighbors and you love the sense of community you feel, greeting them in the morning as you sit on the front steps eating your cereal, watching the passersby and feeling fortunate that you are not one of the people who has to find a parking space because you have a driveway, one block from the beach.

On the beach you play with your friend Niki and you both know about the different kinds of sand, the main ingredient in the pastries you make when you play bakery. You decorate your cakes by sprinkling dry white sand on them like sugar and topping them with little purple wildflowers that grow in the dunes. You play mermaids in the water. You don't care that the water is cold. You don't even feel the cold, especially if you have your boogie board. You run in as fast as you can and you feel strong and brave and fearless.

You know that the ocean has different moods. There are "lake days" when there are no waves at all. Those days the water is usually warmer and lighter blue. There are days when the water is very dark blue and you know that means the water will be very cold. Some days you can see your feet at the bottom. Other days the water is full of seaweed. You know that in the afternoon the wind changes and white caps appear. You know it is better to be on the beach early.

In July you know that you have to combat the greenheads. When they bite you it hurts. You are vigilant and you are patient and you let them land on you and then you smack them and watch them drop dead on the sand and you feel satisfaction. You know they will be gone by August. But, you know that in August the red seaweed comes. You don't like the seaweed but you don't let it stop you either. You still go in the water; you just don't open your eyes underneath. There is nothing to see anyway.

After the beach you take your shower in the outside shower. Before stepping under the water, you can smell the sun and the salt on your body. This is a very good smell. If it is in the afternoon, around three o'clock, the sun shines in and creates rainbows in the water all around you. After your shower, you sit on the back deck and soak in a little more sun before going inside to get dressed. You watch the weeping willows at the back of the yard swaying in the breeze and you know that weeping willows are one of the most beautiful kinds of tree. You want to swing on their branches but you know that you can't because they are not strong enough. You still imagine how fun it would be, if they could hold you.

You go for fourteen mile bike rides along the whole length of the beach and back. Scarborough to Old Orchard to Ocean Park to Kinney Shores to Saco to Camp Ellis. If it is high tide you stop and jump off the bridge between Ocean Park and Kinney Shores. You sneak into Ferry Beach State Park and you ride on the trails in the woods, on the boardwalks and over the little bridges. Later, you might sit on the front porch and read your book, accompanied by your parents, everyone sitting on rocking chairs and reading together but separately. You enjoy this quiet family time.

At night you might go to Old Orchard and go on some rides.

You definitely have pier fries smothered in ketchup and vinegar. This is a delicacy as delicious as anything you might eat in a Michelin-starred restaurant. This is a fact. You go for ice cream where the portions are large and generous and the prices are low and you stress over what flavor to choose. This is the most stressful thing in your life.

Sometimes you take a break from the beach and you go with your parents to visit their friends who spend their summers on the lake. You wonder if you had to choose between the lake and the ocean which one you would pick, and you enjoy weighing the pros and cons as you drive up to Sebago alone in the backseat. You know that the lake doesn't have seaweed and that it is generally warmer than the ocean, but you know that the bottom can be slimy. You also know that there are black flies at the lake and sometimes those fly right into your mouth and get caught in your throat and you know this is very, very unpleasant. At the lake you take the canoe out all by yourself. You can canoe all the way to that island off in the distance and you know that there is just nothing to worry about because you are wearing a life jacket. When you are done exploring the lake in the canoe, the next item on your agenda is to lay on the hammock and look up at the trees and listen to the adults talk until it is time to go back home.

On the Fourth of July, you go to the parade. The parade starts at nine o'clock in the morning. If you get there at 9:05, you will have missed it. You walk down to the parade route with your parents with plenty of time because your mom is always anxious about being late. The parade is the only thing for which you have ever seen your mom be anxious about being late. You love the parade and are excited and giddy to watch it. You normally don't even like parades, but this parade is different. This parade is the most under-achieving parade you have ever seen and the laziness and absurdity of this parade makes you laugh and cry for the entire five whole minutes it lasts. There is usually a bagpiper. And a fire truck. And an oil truck. And kids on bikes. Some have been decorated in red, white and blue. Some haven't been decorated at all. There are dogs that may have a red, white or blue bandana around their neck... or not. One year there is a horse. As the parade passes by, the onlookers join the parade, and in the end the parade is basically the whole community just walking down the middle of the street together to the fire station where the Ladies' Auxiliary serves strawberry shortcake and you can have as many servings as you want because they never seem to run out.

In the fall you get to see the leaves change every color. You know which trees on your way to school turn the brightest orange. You know that in the mornings frost covers the grass and the air is crisp. You walk to school and you are tempted to touch the bushes with the burrs as you pass them. Why do you want to touch those burrs? You know what happens when you do - you have burrs stuck in your fingers for the rest of the day and they are annoying to pick out. But you touch the burrs anyway. You don't know what compels you to do this.

On Halloween, you take turns each year going trick or treating in your neighborhood or Joanna's. You use pillowcases to collect the candy because you are very ambitious and take this holiday very seriously. You weigh your candy-filled bedding at the end of the night, hoping for a number that beat the previous year's that will then serve as your goal to beat the following year. You are methodical about separating and making trades. You will gladly give up Smarties or Nerds for Reese's peanut butter cups but no one ever wants to get rid of those. Though Joanna lives in a different town from you and goes to a different school, you have known each other since you were three years old. You spend almost every weekend either at her house or she at yours. You prefer hers because she has siblings and you don't. You are never alone in the backseat if Susan is herding you all somewhere, usually to watch Joanna's brother play hockey. You know all the hockey players in Cape Elizabeth. You have crushes on most of them, but her brother Daniel is your favorite. He is very, very cool. Daniel introduced you to Run DMC and you know every word of every song from their *1984* album by heart. He is younger than you but you look up to him. You want to emulate his sense of humor. You learn to be funnier from him. You learn about what jokes of yours fall flat and are better left unsaid.

Thanksgiving is spent at your grandparents' in Lewiston. The blueberry and raspberry bushes are dead for the winter, the pear and apple trees are naked. The garden is under a blanket of snow. Your grandmother prepares the Thanksgiving meal. It is served on china and has many courses, always starting with chopped liver and sweet and sour meatballs. You regret never getting the recipe for the meatballs; they were so delicious. You never got the recipe for her split pea soup either but you were able to figure that one out for yourself later. Your grandmother calls lunch "dinner" and dinner "supper." They keep kosher so you can't have a glass of milk to wash down your meal. This is extremely dissatisfying to you.

In Lewiston, your grandparents live in the same house in which your grandmother grew up. It is a three story, three family home. When your grandmother was little, she and her sister lived on the first floor with your great-grandparents. When Auntie Ada got married, she moved to the second floor. When your grandmother got married, she moved to the third. Your dad grew up with the whole family under one roof, his cousins downstairs, his grandparents too. You spend Thanksgiving at separate tables from your cousins, as they ate at Auntie Ada's downstairs. But, before and after the meal there is lots of running up and down the stairs, in and out of each home, until it is time to drive back to Portland and you lay looking up at the stars, alone in the backseat.

40 A Manicure Might Have Saved My Life

One of the reasons I am glad I am from Maine is that I think there is a certain genuineness, friendliness and openness in Mainers. We smile at people on the street. We know our neighbors. When I moved to DC people seemed so cold and unfriendly to me. People do not talk on the metro. They do not smile on the street. And they *certainly* don't talk to you in elevators. When my parents visit me and we take the elevator up to my apartment, they always talk to whomever is in it with us. I probably turn bright red because this is not how things are done here. I feel a kinship to other Mainers, like Eric, though I meet very few in DC. Actually, I get excited about anyone I meet who is from New England. Finding out that Kate was from Vermont made me confident to be my most friendly Maine self when I met her.

I had just been out in LA visiting my cousin James and his wife Nicole. I had never been to LA before and I wanted to have a local experience, not a touristy one. I just wanted to do what they would do anyway, in their normal lives. The day I arrived, they were also arriving from a vacation in New Zealand. Since we were all pretty tired from our trips, we wanted to just stay low key. Nicole suggested that we go get manicures. There was nothing special about the place we went, but I still felt glamorous, getting a manicure, in LA. I had never had a gel manicure before, nor really hardly any manicures before. I liked it, so I made the decision to keep up with it when I went back to DC, and it was a decision that changed my life. As I found out later, that decision resulted in the universe aligning for me with a serendipitous twist.

A few weeks later, back in DC, I went for my second manicure. At this time, I was really lonely. I wasn't seeing Nathan anymore. I missed him terribly. Dating was not going well. On top of that, I felt like I had no friends. I would walk around and feel like if I died, no one would even notice and no one would even come to my funeral, aside from my parents. That was such a depressing thought. I was a friendly, nice, outgoing, fun, kind person. Why did no one ever want to ask me to do anything? I had put a lot of effort into forming friendships with people, was always reaching out and inviting people to do things. But, the invitations were never reciprocated, and often when I would invite someone to do something, they would tell me they already had plans. Why didn't they invite me to join them for their plans? I didn't understand. It hurt me. I was very, very lonely. Sometimes I felt such pangs of loneliness that I actually felt a physical discomfort from it, as if my organs were being deprived of oxygen. It was not a happy time. Fridays were the worst. I would have nothing to do on a Friday night and no one to do it with. I wanted to put myself out there, expose myself to the opportunity to meet someone in real life but I had no wingperson. It sucked.

And then I sat down to get a manicure next to Kate. Kate was so, so, so pretty, a petite brunette dressed in lululemon with beautiful brown eyes and the longest eyelashes I had ever seen in my life. Her skin was flawless. She was too pretty to possibly be friendly but I couldn't help commenting on those lashes and asked her if they were real. They were! We started talking and it turned out that she was from Vermont, no wonder she was so open and friendly despite being so darn pretty. I wanted to be best friends immediately. We friended each other on Facebook before saying goodbye and I was so happy/relieved/excited that she seemed open to being my badly needed friend.

It turned out that Kate needed a friend too and from that point on we were inseparable. She listened to me go on and on about Nathan. She laughed at my dating stories and jokes. She gave good advice and was empathetic. She acted like the president of my fan club, constantly telling me how amazing and funny and beautiful I am. She was everything I could have asked for in a best friend. The best part was that Kate knew how to hang. Not many people I have met in DC know how to just hang out. People here need an activity. They have to go to happy hour. Or out to dinner. They don't know how to just sit on each other's bedroom floors for hours and hours just talking. Kate knew how to do that. She changed my life. I wasn't lonely for a best friend anymore after meeting Kate.

The most serendipitous thing about meeting Kate, that we didn't discover until a year later, was that growing up in Vermont, Kate actually lived *across the street* from my cousin James. James, who I was visiting in LA. James, whose wife I went with to get my first gel manicure. James, who if I hadn't visited, I wouldn't have gotten a gel manicure and I wouldn't have met Kate - Kate who lived *across the street from James*. It blew our minds when we found this out.

The other incredible thing is that this didn't just happen with Kate. When I was in LA, I also went to Equinox gym with Nicole. I really liked it, so I decided to see about joining Equinox when I got back. That is where I met Cat, who worked in membership sales. Cat from Scotland with the very blonde hair and the very blue eyes and the very long eyelashes, coincidentally, just as long as Kate's. She was so friendly and open. I liked her immediately. Cat, who, like Kate, also knows how to hang, and who knows how to be a friend, extending herself, checking in, being a good and caring listener. Cat with the very nice husband Matt who now helps me with beverages when I have a dinner party. I am so grateful that I found Cat who I also needed to be best friends with from the moment that I met her.

Thank you to James for marrying Nicole and inviting me to LA and thank you to Nicole for taking me to get manicures and taking me to Equinox and for saving me from loneliness. You just never know what can happen, whose orbit you will cross that will change your life or save it.

41 Long-Distance Platonic Life Partners

Before Kate and Cat there was Manal. Manal was my Kate before Kate. She was the first person I had met in a long time who knew how to hang. How I miss Manal! She is one of the people on my long list of people I love who left. That list started out with my family's best friends, first Ken and Starr and then the Mazers. Ken and Starr were like second parents to me. But, when I was in sixth grade they sat me down and told me they were moving to

Texas. That was devastating news; they broke my heart. And then the Mazers, our other best friends, moved to California when I was in high school. Our families had always been together. They had two sons, Jonathan and David. Jonathan and I were born eight days apart. We knew each other our entire lives. My family would go to their house on the weekends or they would come to ours and we'd just *be* together. My dad and David and Jonathan's dad would sprawl out, each on an opposite end of either their L-shaped couch or ours, and they'd fall asleep. I always thought it was so funny how they'd nap "together." But they left.

It happened again when I moved to DC and I had the best boss in the whole world, Beth. I loved Beth. She and her husband John were like my new Ken and Starr. They had me over for Christmas one year, inviting me into their home for a sleepover. It was my first time celebrating the holiday that had plagued my Jewish childhood. We had a delicious Christmas Eve dinner that Beth prepared and they even hung a stocking up for me and gave me presents in the morning. They made me feel like family and I loved them for their warmth and inclusiveness. And then they left too. They moved to Chicago. Jodi replaced Beth and was just as cool. Everyone wanted to be around Jodi. And then Jodi moved to California. It felt like everyone I loved always left. But Manal, ooof, her leaving was the icing on the loneliness cake.

My orbit crossed with Manal's when we both took an American Red Cross International Humanitarian Law class together. I couldn't believe how pretty she was, and, always in search of a best friend, I asked her if she wanted to have lunch with me on our lunch break. She was exotic looking, a Lebanese Canadian, in the U.S. because of her husband. One of those girls with perfect hair, perfect makeup, perfect eyeliner, perfect face, perfect outfit. I am not one of those girls. I try, but even *thinking* about attempting to use a curling iron exhausts me. I admire those girls.

We had lunch together in the cafeteria and an hour was clearly not enough time to adequately delve into all the topics we were rapidly covering. We ended up talking right off the bat about some very personal things, like my divorce. It had been awhile since I had had a heart to heart like that and it was obvious that the conversation needed to continue after the one-day class was over. She asked me a lot of questions and was friendly. She was direct, which I liked, but also maybe a bit too blunt. She flat out told me she didn't care for my hairstyle. *Jeez. Thanks.* You have to have a thick skin with Manal but you always know where you stand and never need to worry about her being fake. We exchanged numbers and planned on seeing each other again the next week. I hoped that she would approve of my hair the next time I saw her.

The next week we met for a movie date. Manal didn't like the movie. She had a lot of opinions about things she didn't like and she didn't hold back from sharing them. She reminded me of a younger, less diplomatic version of myself. I wasn't sure if I liked this girl. She seemed negative. But, she kept wanting to hang out with me and I desperately needed a friend and no one else was soliciting my companionship. I figured I'd give her one more try. The next weekend she invited me to spend the day with her, get pedicures, go out for lunch. I agreed, hesitantly, trepidatiously.

On our third meeting, Manal finally opened up to me and confided in me that she was getting a divorce. Now it made more sense why she had given off such a negative vibe. She was devastated that her marriage was ending. I think she had latched onto me because she knew I had been through it, that I would understand and that I could provide guidance to her for getting through it herself. Once she opened up to me and let me in, we quickly became very close friends, best friends. I was glad to have someone to support, to give back what Quique had given me, to be useful.

I knew that in the end, her divorce was going to break my heart as well because Manal would have to go back to Canada since she didn't have a work visa. In the time we had left, Manal and I spent as much of it together as possible. There were sleepovers at her place or mine. She wanted to be with me constantly. It was so nice. If I was at her place, she did not want me to leave. Maybe it was partially because she didn't want to be alone, but it wasn't just that. She liked my company. I liked hers as well, loved it, in fact. That felt good and was such a welcome respite from being plagued by the loneliness I so often experienced.

And then the dreaded time came that Manal had to go back to Canada. The plan was that her husband was going to drop her off at the airport, bid her a final farewell and she was going to fly home. I knew this type of goodbye would have made the crushing blow of the situation even worse and would have prolonged her healing process. I remembered how I had cried the entire flight home when I left Quique in Spain and we hadn't really even been boyfriend and girlfriend. This was an end to a *marriage*. I told her, "No way." I was going to Florida to visit my parents, so I suggested she have her husband drop her off with me and come to Florida instead, spend a few days in the sunshine, get a little distance from her broken heart, and *then* go back. That was a much better plan for her mental health, so that is what she did.

Beautiful Lebanese Canadian Manal, hair all the way down her back, perfectly made up, perfect body, perfect everything Manal. I look like a slob next to her in all the pictures from that trip. I don't even care. She was so glamorous and beautiful; I was entertained just looking at her. Every night we would sit on my bed together going through the pictures from the day, deciding which ones were good enough to post in our Facebook album. When we had to bring her to the airport it was such a sad goodbye - for her, for me, for us. She was leaving a life behind and we were both losing the proximity of our best friend.

She struggled when she went back to Canada. She was devastated that her marriage ended, she was angry that she had put her career on hold for nothing and was starting back on the bottom despite having a Masters. She felt deceived and confused and she missed the life she had made in Virginia, her apartment, her independence - now she was back living with her parents. She had a lot to work through. Poor Manal. I offered my support, empathy and advice and I listened to her cry and reminded her that someday she would eventually feel better. However, Manal wasn't one to feel sorry for herself; she didn't just want a sympathetic ear - she wanted advice. She was actively trying to heal and I was impressed by her strength and her attitude. She made me feel wise and useful and helpful. It was flattering to be listened to and consulted and it was nice to be needed.

That spring Manal joined me and my parents again for a week in Paris. She painstakingly selected her outfits each day, choosing what to wear depending on where we were going, so that in the photos she would have the right outfit for the right place. After ending up at the Eiffel Tower spontaneously one day, for the rest of the trip Manal lamented, "I can't believe I didn't have a better outfit for the Eiffel Tower!" Her vexed dissatisfaction made me laugh, though I did offer heartfelt sympathy. She influenced me in this way, and I am now better about selecting my outfits and planning for touristic photo shoots. It is fun to be glamorous on vacation, or, well, anytime.

Manal and I share a love of beautiful things - fashion, decor, flowers, a beautifully set table. She says that we are aesthetically sensitive. I am so glad that she coined that phrase because she is so right – it has helped explain a lot about me! I have always been aesthetically sensitive, my awareness of proportion and symmetry and layout has accompanied me my whole life. When I was little, my dad built me a doll house, a wonderful doll house which I loved. However, the proportions of the doll house were too large for normal dollhouse furniture, making the rooms appear slightly too large or the furniture slightly too small. I remember this bothering me, yet I was no more than three years old.

When I was young and home sick from school one day, my mom brought me some magazines to entertain me. Did she bring me *Tiger Beat* or *17*? No. I didn't want those. Instead, she brought me *House and Garden* and *House Beautiful*. I was in *sixth grade*. I dreamed of someday having a home where everything was white, the color only coming from the fresh flowers I would have in vases all around.

Manal appreciated my eye for decor and her frequent calls to me from Canada included decorating consultations or complaints about how frustrated we were that the distance kept us from having each other at our dinner parties with our beautifully set tables because no one else appreciated them as much as we did. Our running joke was to lament the fact that we were not lesbians, which prevented us from just getting married so that she could get her green card and we could be together. That would have solved our distance problems, our dating problems and our dinner party problems. But, since we are not, we must be satisfied with at least being "long-distance platonic life partners," another term she coined for us. So, that is what we are.

42 Welcome to Lebanon

Happily, Manal found someone to be more than just platonic with and she ended up marrying him in Lebanon four years after we met. Of course, I was invited to the wedding. A wedding in Lebanon!! At first I was hesitant to go because, well, it was in Lebanon. The Middle East? And I'm Jewish? But, I calculated my risks and I put fear aside and I bought a ticket. And, once again, I felt that sensation of being the luckiest girl in the world, getting to see another country with people who were *from* there, integrating myself into yet another family, a houseguest on yet another continent. Manal's family joined my list of families who have welcomed me into their home - my French host family, my Argentine host family, my Italian host family and Alejandro's family - they all made me feel like I was one of them.

This time family time was in the mountains of Hasbaya, Lebanon. Family breakfasts were eaten on the terrace overlooking the morning sunlight on the mountains, Lebanese breakfasts of cucumber and peppers and tomatoes and olives and pita bread with lebne or manakish topped with zaatar, accompanied by fresh-squeezed orange juice from oranges we picked ourselves.

When I first arrived in Lebanon, we spent our first two days in Beirut at the Phoenicia, a beautiful five-star hotel, our room overlooking the Mediterranean. Our hotel was in a very modern, elegant, and posh section of the city. So, it was quite shocking to my privileged and sheltered American eyes to see right next to our hotel, the infamous Holiday Inn, unofficial monument to the civil war, a building pockmarked and scarred with bullet holes and holes from something much bigger than bullets. Thirty-five years after the war, the bombed out wreckage remains an eyesore, 26 stories of prime real estate, wasted due to bureaucracy and infighting between the owners. The juxtaposition of our five-star hotel next to this carcass of a building couldn't have welcomed me to Lebanon better than a *Welcome to Lebanon, Jennifer* sign.

My best photo from the trip I took while lying at the Phoenicia pool, a luxurious oasis filled with giant planters and balustrades and glamorous people lounging about, drinking cocktails, maybe smoking hookahs. In the photo there is the pool in the foreground and in the background on the left and right are the Phoenicia Hotel buildings flanking the Holiday Inn skeleton in the middle. I just happened to snap the shot as a waiter's tray carrying a bottle of Moët & Chandon champagne entered the frame. The photo is a perfect example of how the beautiful views in Lebanon are often ruined by wreckage, rubble, and litter. It says to me, "Now let's drink champagne as we ignore that which is right in front of our eyes." Welcome to Lebanon.

The first thing you notice when you land in Beirut is the litter on the sides of the exit ramp as you leave the plane. I had never seen trash on an airplane ramp before and there wasn't just a little. Either various people who had just gotten off the plane before me had treated the ramp as their personal trash can or the airport workers were just too apathetic to pick up the accumulation over time. Either way, it wasn't a very warm or impressive welcome to the country. The next thing you notice, as an American, is the non-air-conditioned air as you enter the airport arrivals section which looks like it has not had one single update since it was originally built thirty years ago. Next, I waited in an incredibly long and slow line to get through passport control, entertaining myself by observing the other arrivals. Some women were covered from head to toe in that oppressive, AC-free heat. I could NEVER.

My parents and my American friends who had never been to a Middle Eastern country were concerned about my safety while there. "Don't tell anyone you've been to Israel if they ask!" I have never been to Israel, so that was easy. My dad told me, "Don't act so American when you are there! Don't be loud! Don't be enthusiastic! Don't smile at anyone! Act like you are a Russian - don't smile at strangers! Don't tell anyone you are Jewish!"

Well, not one person asked me if I had been to Israel, no one asked me my religious background, and well, sorry, I can't help it - I smile at everyone. I just do. I tried not to. But, even at one of the military checkpoints, I couldn't help smiling at the guy holding the AK-47 as he waved us through. Oops. Maybe it was because I was with my hosts the whole time, or maybe it is just because I am ignorant, but at no moment did I feel unease while there.

Before I left for my trip, my parents wanted to know my itinerary and all the places I would be. I asked Manal to send me the addresses. She told me that in Lebanon there are no street addresses, just town names. I found this very hard to believe but I got confirmation that it was true when we were in Beirut and we took a taxi to meet her cousins out for a drink at a bar called Coop d'Etat. All we could give the taxi driver was the street name and the neighborhood and then once we got nearby we had to stop various people on the street for directions to the exact location. Welcome to Lebanon.

Manal's family is from a town called Hasbaya which is an hour and a half from Beirut. As we drove from Beirut to Hasbaya through the beautiful, mountainous landscape under a bright blue sky, I noticed litter everywhere. Every view of something beautiful had garbage in it. Why? Do they not care about their country? Is it PTSD from years of war? Is it collective depression? Rebellion? It was pervasive almost everywhere I went. I didn't understand it and I didn't get an explanation.

Before leaving for Lebanon, I had not done any research for my trip because I wanted to go with no agenda, for me, the most relaxing way to travel. I am always trying to replicate my arrival in Venice that first time so I just wanted to be surprised. As someone with Arab friends and someone who pays attention to the news, I am aware of conflict in that region. I mean, I have read Tom Friedman's *From Beirut to Jerusalem* so I wasn't going there with total ignorance. But, as I sat on the beach with Niki before leaving for my trip, she kept telling me I needed to read up on where I was going. So, I finally googled "Is Lebanon safe?" the day before I was supposed to leave and the State Department's website made me seriously question my decision. Not only is there a travel warning, but they strongly advise you to stay away from the Syrian border, southern Lebanon which contains Hezbollah territory and the Israeli border. Well, little did I know that Manal's parents' home is eight miles from Damascus, we could *see* Israel on our excursions and we drove right through Hezbollah territory on our way to Hasbaya, which I was very disappointed to learn after the fact that I had slept through.

We spent three days in Hasbaya, a potentially beautiful place, incredibly fertile, yet covered in litter. Bougainvillea and oleander grow everywhere, the roads are lined with purple thistle-like flowers. The hillsides are dotted with olive groves. In Manal's family's neighborhood I saw grapes, figs, oranges, pears, apples, walnuts, pomegranates, persimmons, plums, grapefruits and tomatoes growing in people's yards. Fertile anarchy. It looked like the concept of landscape architecture had not yet been introduced here. Everything just grew haphazardly. Eggplants popped up next to orange trees on her family's land. Neat rows of olive trees growing in olive groves as my French family's house had overlooked? No, more like a jumble of olive trees. Fertile mess dotted everywhere with litter. Welcome to Lebanon.

Hasbaya is a small town of no more than 6,000 people. It seemed like at least half of them were related to Manal because everywhere we went I heard "Oh, yeah, that's my cousin." I loved that. The roads in Hasbaya are incredibly narrow and most can only fit one car through at a time. The town is also in the mountains, so it is incredibly hilly. At first, driving up and down roads that seemed to be, and I am not exaggerating, at a sixty degree angle was terrifying, way more terrifying than Hezbollah territory. I don't even *ski* down trails that steep. You constantly have to beep your horn around every turn in case someone is coming. And, given how curvy the roads are because of the hills, you are beeping your horn literally every five seconds. If you happen to be in an area where the road is just wide enough for two cars going in opposite directions to pass each other, you do so carefully, at the slowest speed possible, which also enables you to say hello to the driver you are passing, who you almost certainly know and are probably related to, shaking hands with each other out the window and mumbling some warm greetings before you are out of earshot.

Lebanon is a country made up of people who mostly identify with one of three religions - Muslim, Christian, and Druze. Manal's family is Druze and their town is a mostly Druze town. Religious Druze people have their own traditional way of dressing. The women wear modest black dresses and cover their heads with a long white head covering. Sometimes they wrap it around so that it covers their mouths as well, but they don't seem to be overly committed to keeping it covering their faces consistently. The men are all mustachioed and wear little white knit caps and also dress all in black. Their pants are baggy in the crotch until about the knee and then taper and are tight at the ankle. I longed to take a picture of them but I knew they were not out and about to satisfy my curiosity and desire to capture their image; they were just living their lives and I didn't want to be intrusive.

In fact, when I was in Lebanon, there was a lot of sensitivity around photography. I was constantly being told by Manal's brother when it was and when it was not safe to take photos. If we were near Hezbollah territory, my camera needed to be put away. Near Israel? *Don't take pictures. Don't take photos of the checkpoints. Don't take photos of people's houses if they are looking.* One person even stopped us one day right in Hasbaya to ask why we were walking around taking photos. There seemed to be a lot of paranoia in this place. Hezbollah spies? Israeli spies? Lebanon seems to be a free-for-all with no actual freedom. Or, as Manal's cousin put it in Beirut when I asked him what was the best and the worst aspect of Lebanon, he said "I have total freedom to do whatever I want... but it's a fucking jungle."

A lot of sitting on terraces is done in Hasbaya. You visit a family member or a friend and you sit on their terrace and look out at the sunset over the mountains and someone brings you a glass of cold lemonade with orange blossom water and serves a tray of an assortment of nuts, dried fruits, and sweets. At Manal's aunt's house, we sat with her on her terrace and drank her lemonade, ate raisins that she had dried herself from her own grapes and munched on almonds and walnuts rolled up in figs. What an experience. I just wish I didn't hate orange blossom water!

The day we arrived in Hasbaya, Manal's mom had a feast ready and prepared for us. She made stuffed grape leaves, stuffed zucchini, homemade french fries and tabbouleh salad. I don't even like stuffed grape leaves and I could not get enough of hers. And, eating french fries WITH tabbouleh salad as apparently these are supposed to be combined and eaten in the same bite? One of the best things I have ever eaten. I sat at the head of the table, with this Lebanese Canadian family, eating this delicious, homemade food and felt once again that I couldn't believe this was my life.

Manal's family was so warm and welcoming to me. They showered me with hospitality and I soaked it all up. I loved it. Fresh-squeezed orange juice in the mornings, Manal's brother taking me on outings, constantly worrying if I was seeing enough of the sights, trying enough of the foods. On shorter excursions, Manal wanted me to sit in the front seat of the car so I would have the best view, despite her tendency to get carsick. They didn't let me spend a penny of my own money, and I reveled in being treated as one should be treated when one is a guest. I felt at home, not just because they made me feel at home, but because I identified with them, for I'd like to think that is how I treat guests in my own home. Hospitality is something I value. It made me feel so happy and grateful to be on the receiving end, and I hoped that someday they would visit me so that I could return the gesture with the same warmth and generosity that they had offered me.

The strangest thing I observed in Hasbaya was that everyone drinks mate (pronounced mah-tay), brought back from Argentina at some point by some member of the Lebanese Druze community.

Mate is a tea-like beverage made out of the dried leaves of a tree native to the jungles along the Paraná river in South America. It is served in a gourd and sipped through a silver straw that has a filter at the bottom. One person, the server, puts the mate in the gourd and then fills it with almost boiling water. The gourd is then passed back and forth between each person partaking and the server who refills the water each time. Each person gets a turn to drink, all sharing from the same gourd and straw. How did this American girl from Maine end up in two places on opposite sides of the earth where mate is served? If not for my time in Santa Fe, Argentina where I was introduced to both mate and my ex-husband, I might not have found myself on a terrace in Hasbaya, Lebanon because Manal and I wouldn't have had our divorces over which to bond. As the mate was passed around the table, it made me want to write a PhD dissertation comparing and contrasting Santa Fe, Argentina with Hasbaya, Lebanon. I think the only one interested in that topic, however, would be me. But, maybe not…

There I sat, one evening on their terrace, enjoying a tray of snacks and the balmy air and the stars overhead in the clear, dark sky, politely listening, yet not understanding a word, as the family and a neighbor of theirs visited in Arabic. Not an English speaker, yet wanting to be inclusive, the gentleman happened to ask me if I spoke Spanish. I don't know how it occurred to him to ask me that, but of course I said yes and thus we proceeded to converse in fluent Spanish which he had learned while living in Venezuela. And where did he tell me his son happened to be living at the moment? Argentina. Santa Fe, to be exact!

Sometimes the universe just blows my mind.

My trip to Lebanon culminated in our stay in Deir El Qamar, a beautiful little town with narrow, cobblestone streets, much less litter, and a gorgeous hotel with a courtyard where I just wanted to sit and watch the light pass through all day long as Monet did with the subjects of his paintings. My favorite college professor used to give tours of Washington, DC, one of which included the National Gallery of Art where he would point out two side-by-side paintings of Monet's *Rouen Cathedral* and tell us, "He wasn't painting the cathedral. He was painting the *light* on the cathedral." I never forgot that and I often do the same thing with my photography - I try to capture the light.

So, now I found myself in the Deir Al Oumara hotel in Deir El Qamar, in Lebanon, in the Middle East. The hotel was formerly a palace built in the early 1800's. The palace has a square courtyard which is enclosed on three sides by Ottoman and Florentine styled arcades and on the fourth offers a breathtaking view of the mountains, behind which the sun sets. In the middle of the courtyard is a simple and elegant octagonal fountain, surrounded by rustic wood tables scattered among teal blue metal ones. It just couldn't have been any prettier. I didn't even want to sightsee. I just wanted to plant myself at a table in the shade and enjoy the view of the courtyard, the fountain, the mountains and the light.

The wedding took place in an outdoor venue in a nearby town. I was so excited to go to a Lebanese wedding. I had seen pictures of one before; the women were all made up like movie stars, everyone looking so glamorous. I couldn't wait to see that with my own eyes, and Manal's friends and family did not disappoint. Manal's cousin Kinda wore a full length cerulean blue gown with matching eyeliner and glitter outlining her eyes. I never knew how badly I needed a cerulean blue gown and eye glitter before seeing Kinda.

As the bride and groom made their entrance and everyone surrounded them on the dance floor for the first dance, the sun had set and the sky over the mountains was bright orange. We danced to Arabic music celebrating the bride and groom; there I was, an American Jew surrounded by Lebanese Druze Arabs, dancing, and thinking that it was one of the most special moments of my life. It's pretty amazing - I have now attended weddings in four countries on four continents.

The next day, sadly, it was time for me to go back to the States. Manal and her new husband drove me back to the airport in Beirut, and once again I found myself alone in the backseat.

Well... that is a lie. But, it would have been really good for this book's narrative. The truth is, I wasn't really alone. I was in the backseat with Manal's mother-in-law. Oh well. Metaphorically alone.

After a teary goodbye with Manal, having now shared time in our third country together, not knowing when we would see each other again, I composed myself for the task of navigating the departure section of the Beirut airport which, apparently, is just as bad as the arrival section. The signage is horrible - you don't have any way to know if you are supposed to go through the East or West Security sides and the fact that they have various signs pointing this choice out makes it seem like it is a very important choice. However, you can only guess which is correct, because there is no other way to know. Similarly, there is also no counter for Air Emirates, nor is there any signage to let you know that if you are flying Air Emirates you are actually supposed to check in for your flight at Middle East Airlines counter number 47. I guess it makes sense that it would be this way in a country where they do not have addresses and you have to ask for directions whenever you need to get somewhere new.

Also, apparently there are no bathrooms on the ticket level, which means you have to take your forty pound suitcase up the escalator to the bathroom and then bounce it back down the stairs, hoping a wheel won't break, as apparently there is not a down escalator either, and, obviously, no sign pointing you in the direction of an elevator.

Luckily, the airport does have WiFi which you can use for free for thirty minutes. Once you have used up your free thirty minutes, you have to log on with a user ID and password. Unfortunately, however, there is no way to procure either of these. That is a shame because it means you only have WiFi for one third of the amount of time it takes you to wait at counter 47 and to go through passport control. Given how slow the passport control lines are, it seems as if they want you to neither enter nor leave the country. Welcome to Lebanon.

After getting to spend time again with Manal, it was hard saying goodbye once again, knowing that we'd have to go back to our long distance relationship. When she had first left the States, we talked on the phone almost every single day. That summer following her return to Canada, Manal came to visit me in Maine. It was so great to be reunited with her again, go for bike rides with her, lay on the beach with her, have a best friend near me. It had meant so much to me that she paid for an expensive plane ticket and flew all the way from Edmonton, Canada to see me, when in DC I couldn't get people who lived within five miles and the cost of a metro fare to hang out with me. She had left a void in DC that I needed filled, badly. For a brief moment she had been with me and I had a best friend to do things with, someone who wanted to spend time with me. But, then I was back to walking past restaurants filled with people and feeling like I was on the outside again. I was back to awful Friday nights with no invitations or companionship.

Until I met Kate. And Cat. I also started hanging out more with my neighbor Rajiv. And then I met my neighbor Noora at the pool and we became inseparable. I also met Annya and Greg and a second Rajiv and Julie there. And then I reconnected with newly single Agnes (roommate #50) who I had adored. And my job sent me to a conference where I met Jared. And Noora introduced me to Marie. And I also became close with Randa (roommate #55) and Dena (roommate #58), sisters who lived with me at separate times and who both became some of my favorite people. And, all of a sudden I had friends. And I introduced my friends to each other and my friends became friends. And finally, *finally* I had a group of friends. And I wasn't lonely anymore. I didn't have the husband I had wanted or the family I had dreamed of and wished for and I didn't have Nathan, but I wasn't on the outside looking in. I was on the inside. And that feels so much better. And now, when Noora and I uber downtown to meet our friends for a night out, I am not alone in the backseat anymore.

43 *The End*

Without even meaning to, Nathan added so many positive things to my life. When I was dating him, we were *just* dating. He wasn't my *boyfriend,* but he was all I could think about and therefore I needed to distract myself. So, I started going out a ton, meeting new people, and doing lots of activities. My life became so much more exciting. Before I met him, I just spent hours and hours and hours watching TV. My DVR was the most stressful thing in my life. I stressed over how I would accomplish watching all the things I had recorded. I stressed over it so much that watching TV and getting through my DVR was actually something I considered *productive*. Who puts watching TV as a chore on their to-do list?! I was compulsive about watching the news. I actually DVR'd the news! I couldn't miss an "episode." Even if I went away on vacation, I would have to come back and compulsively catch up on watching the *news*. Sometimes, I would have to watch up to fourteen "episodes!" That was very time consuming! It was ridiculous! After I met Nathan, I couldn't focus on TV anymore. I went cold turkey on DVRing the news. Now, I don't DVR anything. I can barely even sit on the couch anymore; I am too busy being out and about, actually living life (which is so much better), and I have my path crossing with Nathan's to thank for that.

Nathan was my rejection mentor. He was a man whose ways I could incorporate into my own rejection arsenal, but who I could also look up to and respect for his honesty and straightforwardness and say YES, there ARE men out there who possess these qualities and I know that because I know HIM.

I also got Imaginary Nathan who I used to cope with not talking to Real Nathan but who also distracts me from anyone else I might be dating and upset over. That actually helped a lot. Having Nathan be the one I missed and was frustrated over helped me deal with all the other dating disappointments. Who cares that some guy who was Not Nathan blew me off when he wasn't really who I wanted to be with anyway?

Also, given that I was single and had no one to love, it would have been hard to not have a specific direction to which I could point all the love I have in my heart. As I told him once:

> no one makes me feel the feelings you make me feel and they are such good feelings, even if I still never see you in real life. you make me feel so happy, you make me feel the blood in my veins

I could say nice things to you for hours on end
and never run out and that makes me feel so happy to
feel that way about someone

By no means did Nathan put any effort into having any of
these positive influences on me. They just happened as a result of
our orbits crossing paths - that plus my determination to focus on
and extract the positive from people, situations and frustrations,
enabled by my attitude of gratitude. It didn't work out as I would
have liked, but I am still very grateful he swiped right on me.

And that I got to see him that one last time.

Nathan. I wanted to tell you that it did me so good to see you.
You should know that it had a such a positive impact on me and
I am so grateful. I was feeling pretty down before I saw you. I
wasn't feeling great about my looks or hopeful that I would ever
find someone or even hopeful in general. I did not really expect
to ever seen you again and then all of a sudden, there you were,
in my apartment. Seeing you reminded me that you never know
WHAT can happen. Without even being aware of it Nathan, you
brought me back to life. You gave me back my positive energy. So,
I want to thank you. Thank you for making me feel desired and
boosting my confidence. Thank you for taking my breath away
while allowing me to breathe again. Thank you for any attention
you have given me since I met you. You made me feel so much
peace and happiness. You have no idea.

For fifteen months I wondered WHY did God put you in my
path just to have twelve perfect moments and then be frustrated
for the rest of my life? WHY?! What had I done in a past life to
deserve this type of karma? This endless frustration that we are
not together? But then I saw you and that became the catalyst
I had needed to start writing the stories that have been swirling
around in my head for years, which suddenly began pouring out
of me, starting as a love letter to you, words that I had to get out

but did not intend to send. Now when I wonder why I had to go through all that frustration, the answer appears in the form of a book – it seems you were put in my path so that I could finally write these stories. So, thank you. Thank you for being my accidental catalyst.

Even though we are not together, I am so grateful that I did meet you and for those 25 days. And I am pretty sure I will never not love you.

About the Author

Jennifer's life changed with a catalyst on March 15, 2017. Five days later, she sat down to write a love letter and it turned into a book, the first draft of which poured out of her and was completed in 23 days. Becoming a writer or successful blogger was never on her radar and sharing her life and secrets with the entire world (specifically, her parents) was never her intention. You can read more about her at www.aloneinthebackseat.com and see pictures from the stories in this book on her blog and on www.facebook.com/aloneinthebackseat.